LUIGI PIRANDELLO

Born in Sicily in 1867, Pirandello went to university in Palermo and Rome and took a doctorate in Bonn, before settling into the café-bohemian literary life of Rome in the 1890s. In 1894 he married the beautiful daughter of his father's business associate, but after bearing three children her already fragile mental stability was undermined by the financial ruin of both her father and her father-in-law. Pirandello supported his family by taking a university lecturing post – and by writing. Most of his best-known works were written in the shadows of his wife's increasingly dangerous condition, for which she was eventually committed to a mental clinic in 1919.

He first established his reputation with short stories, novels and two philosophical works. Playwriting came fairly late in his career, but it was his plays which won him an international reputation. Amongst his best-known outside Italy are *Right You Are, If You Think So!* (1917), *The Rules of the Game* (1918), *Six Characters in Search of an Author* (1921), which provoked uproar when first staged in Rome but soon came to be seen as seminal, helped by an enormously successful production in Paris in 1924, *Naked* (1922), *Henry IV* (1922), *The Man with the Flower in his Mouth* (1923), *As You Desire Me* (1936) and *The Mountain Giants*, produced a year after his death in Rome in 1936. He won the Nobel Prize for Literature in 1934.

RUPERT GOOLD

Rupert is Artistic Director of Headlong Theatre. Productions for Headlong include *The Last Days of Judas Iscariot*, *Rough Crossings*, *Faustus*, *Restoration* and *Paradise Lost*. He was an Associate Artist at Salisbury Playhouse 1996-97, and from 2002-5, he was Artistic Director of the Royal and Derngate Theatres in Northampton. Other theatre includes: *Macbeth* (Chichester Festival Theatre/Gielgud, West End/Brooklyn Academy of Music/Lyceum, Broadway); *The Glass Menagerie* (Apollo); *The Tempest*, *Speaking Like Magpies* (RSC); *Scaramouche Jones* (national and international tours); *Gone to LA*, *Sunday Father* (Hampstead Theatre); *The Colonel Bird* (Gate); *Hamlet*, *Othello*, *Waiting for Godot*, *Insignificance*, *The Weir*, *Betrayal*, *Arcadia*, *Summer Lightning* (Royal and Derngate Theatres); *The End of the Affair*, *Dancing at Lughnasa*, *Habeas Corpus* (Salisbury Playhouse); *Travels with My Aunt* (Salisbury Playhouse and national tour); *Broken Glass* (Watford Palace); *Privates on Parade* (New Vic); *The Wind in the Willows* (Birmingham Rep). Opera includes: *Le Comte Ory* (Garsington Opera); *L'Opera Seria*, *Gli Equivoci*, *Il Pomo d'Oro* (Batignano).

BEN POWER

Ben is Literary Associate of Headlong Theatre, and co-wrote *Faustus* with Rupert Goold. His work for the stage includes: *A Disappearing Number* for Complicite (international tour and Barbican); the forthcoming *A Tender Thing* for the Royal Shakespeare Company; *Paradise Lost* (Royal Theatre, Northampton and national tour); *Faustus* (Hampstead Theatre); versions of *The Tempest* and *Much Ado About Nothing* for the RSC Complete Works Festival (Swan Theatre and national tours); *Tamburlaine the Great* (Bankside Rose); and *Julius Caesar* (Menier Chocolate Factory). He has acted as dramaturg for Headlong, the RSC, Complicite and Shakespeare's Globe. Current projects include *Gulliver's Travels* for Headlong and a new play for the RSC.

Luigi Pirandello

SIX CHARACTERS IN SEARCH OF AN AUTHOR

in a new version by
Rupert Goold and Ben Power

NICK HERN BOOKS
London
www.nickhernbooks.co.uk

A Nick Hern Book

This version of *Six Characters in Search of an Author* first published in Great Britain as a paperback original in 2008 by Nick Hern Books Limited, 14 Larden Road, London W3 7ST

Six Characters in Search of an Author copyright © 2008 Rupert Goold and Ben Power

Rupert Goold and Ben Power have asserted their right to be identified as the authors of this version

Cover image: Shaun Webb Design, www.swd.uk.com

Cover design: Ned Hoste, 2H

Typeset by Nick Hern Books, London

Printed and bound in Great Britain by CPI Antony Rowe, Chippenham, Wiltshire

A CIP catalogue record for this book is available from the British Library

ISBN   978 1 85459 531 7

FSC

Mixed Sources
Product group from well-managed forests and other controlled sources
Cert no. SGS-COC-2953
www.fsc.org
© 1996 Forest Stewardship Council

'Reality is that which, when you stop
believing in it, doesn't go away'

Philip K. Dick

This version of *Six Characters in Search of an Author* was first performed in a co-production between Chichester Festival Theatre and Headlong Theatre Company, at the Minerva Theatre, Chichester, on 27 June 2008. The cast was as follows:

ACTOR/PIRANDELLO	Jamie Bower
MOTHER	Eleanor David
PRODUCER	Noma Dumezweni
SON	Dyfan Dwyfor
ACTRESS/	
HOUSEKEEPER	Christine Entwisle
STEPDAUGHTER	Denise Gough
CAMERAMAN/	
THEATRE-MAKER B	Jake Harders
RUNNER/	
THEATRE-MAKER A	Jeremy Joyce
EXECUTIVE/MR PACE	John Mackay
FATHER	Ian McDiarmid
GIRL	Freya Parker
EDITOR	Robin Pearce

Director   Rupert Goold
Designer   Miriam Beuther
Lighting Designer   Malcolm Rippeth
Composer and Sound Designer   Adam Cork
Video and Projection Designer   Lorna Heavey

This production subsequently transferred to the Gielgud Theatre, London, on 15 September 2008 (previews from 10 September).

Characters

THE FATHER
THE MOTHER
THE SON
THE STEPDAUGHTER
THE BOY, *twelve years old*
THE GIRL, *ten years old*
PACE, *a pimp*

THE PRODUCER, *a maker of documentary films. Female, mid-thirties*
THE EDITOR
THE ACTOR
THE ACTRESS
THE CAMERAMAN
THE RUNNER
THE EXEC, *a TV commissioning editor*

LULLY, *a Danish doctor*
HANS, *a Danish doctor*
ANDREW, *fourteen years old*
ANDREW'S FATHER
ANDREW'S MOTHER
NURSE
BISHOP, *Philip Ratcliffe, the Bishop of Ely*
THEATRE-MAKER A
THEATRE-MAKER B

Plus various other roles as indicated in the text.

This text went to press before the end of rehearsals and so may differ slightly from the play as performed.

ACT ONE

A large projection screen. On it, a film of a bleak Danish land-scape, which gradually becomes a suburban town. We pass a large, nondescript house, to one side a clutch of pine trees. The camera lingers for a moment, then moves on down a street, past shops and houses, until it arrives at the driveway of a large institutional building. We see a car pull up outside. ANDREW gets out with his PARENTS. A NURSE leaves the building and moves quickly to the car with a wheelchair. ANDREW is very frail as they help him into it.

PRODUCER (*voice-over, mid sentence with film*). ...the drive from Copenhagen airport takes over three hours, but the waiting is at long last over and Andrew arrives at the clinic.

Cut to a middle-aged woman with a Danish accent talking to camera.

LULLY. The final session is always an intense moment for both the patient and all our team at Dignitas.

We see the family move through a waiting room. In the back-ground we see another family, dressed in black, also waiting. The hospital is very clean – pine and pot plants. Occasion-ally we see outside through huge glass windows.

(*Voice-over.*) I wake on these days with a, how d'you say, a... *felag...*

PRODUCER (*voice-over*). Sharper?

LULLY (*voice-over*). Yes. Exactly, a sharper sense of life itself, no? Those days when we are all more in focus – the vivid-ness of the colours in the sky here, the crisp bite of the air.

We see ANDREW sitting at the end of a corridor with his MOTHER, but at a distance and in shadow.

It is a special moment every time. We prepare the room, the bed linen, the lighting, yes, even the injection itself with great consideration and – tenderness, you understand? Even more so for a child, of course. We dream of our perfect wedding, so also we plan our perfect end. This is what we offer, even in cases as tragic as this.

We see a NURSE *place a needle on a bedside table.* ANDREW*'s schoolbag next to the bed. A longer shot of the door to the clinic room. Now* ANDREW'S FATHER *looking at a graveyard. Cut to* ANDREW*'s empty bedroom in Macclesfield, his toys on the floor. Cut back to Denmark and a sudden flock of birds on the horizon. An Arctic hare sits upright in a field. The camera pans mournfully to the sky. Cut back to* LULLY, *dabbing at her eye. Tears.*

I'm sorry. (*Looking away.*) I'm so sorry...

Image freezes. Lights rise on a large modern space, empty. Perhaps it used to be an office, perhaps we see snow falling through a window. In one corner, in darkness, a couple of temporary walls stand, a small film set. To the other side, a temporary editing desk has been set up, with monitors, cables, a control panel and, slightly incongruously, a fishtank. Gathered in front of the screen are the PRODUCER, *her* EDITOR, *an* ACTOR *and an* ACTRESS. *The* EXEC *sits to one side. All wear fleeces and Puffa jackets. Around them are the remains of takeaway food – pastries, sushi and coffees.*

Pause.

PRODUCER. So...

EXEC. Oh... I wonder if...

PRODUCER. Actually, wait. Stu, just lay the track on so Bob can get a better sense of...

EDITOR. Sure. Any bit in partic...?

PRODUCER. No, just the theme.

The entire film plays again on the monitors, this time softly scored with a spare, plaintive piece of music. If one looks closely the second family in black are absent from the film this time.

ACTOR (*about the score*). That's lovely.

ACTRESS. Isn't that the Renault Espace theme?

EDITOR. I don't think so.

The segment finishes again.

EXEC. Okay. So, what's your concern?

PRODUCER. Well, look.

The EDITOR *gets up another piece of footage on a separate screen. It is the unedited* LULLY *interview.*

LULLY. It is a special moment every time. We prepare the room, the bed linen, the lighting, yes, even the injection itself with great consideration and – tenderness, you understand? Even more so for a child, of course. We dream of our perfect wedding so also we plan our perfect end. This is what we offer, even in cases as tragic as this. (*She stops mid-sentence, blinks and then giggles. She dabs at her eye.*) I'm sorry. I'm so sorry. I... (*She laughs again and fiddles at her eye.*) My lens... my contact lens has come loose. There. Better now. Sorry, what was I saying?

The EDITOR *stops the tape. Pause.*

EXEC. I see.

PRODUCER. I mean, it's nothing new, is it? But in the current climate... after Fincham and everything, this whole 'trust' business...

EXEC. Hmm.

PRODUCER. And I'm sure she did have misgivings as well. That the deaths genuinely affected her.

EXEC. Hmm.

PRODUCER. You see, without it we lack a personal response. The whole thing starts to become a bit arid – intellectual positions, pro-life versus pro-choice, etc., etc....

EXEC. Hmm, hmm.

PRODUCER. ...rather than a people piece.

Pause.

EDITOR. Shall I show Bob the, the...

PRODUCER. The, the, the reconstruction, yeah... with the guys.

The EDITOR *brings up another section of tape. Again,* LULLY *speaks to camera.*

LULLY. Of course, our first patient was, well, things were different then, we were just starting and I only had myself and Hans to prepare the barbiturates, but the essence was the same. *Zer gemütlich*, yes. The attention to detail in the moment. So.

We see a reconstruction of this first preparation, with the ACTOR *and the* ACTRESS *playing* LULLY *and* HANS.

ACTOR (*whispering supportively to the* PRODUCER). Looks great, J.

ACTRESS (*moved*). You were right about the wig, you know. It would have been too...

On the monitor we cut back to LULLY, *the camera showing an elderly* HANS *next to her.*

LULLY (*after a smiled beat*). Quite a journey, my friend. Quite a journey together.

HANS *nods gently.*

HANS. It is as the poet Shakespeare says... 'To be or not to be...' (*He chuckles.*) This is the question, no?

Tape stops.

PRODUCER. I mean, that Hamlet thing is probably a red herring, but... you can sense a weight with them...

EXEC. Hmm, hmm.

PRODUCER. And we spoke to her... the doctor... after Andrew's funeral and she was totally choked up...

ACTRESS. Oh God, that was so sad, wasn't it?

EXEC. Do you have that on tape?

PRODUCER. No. They wouldn't let us film in the church.

EXEC. Hmm.

EDITOR (*helpfully*). We could use a cut of some snow melting?

Beat.

PRODUCER. Alternatively, we add some overdubbed text. That's why Fiona's here. Her accent is rock solid.

EXEC. Hmm.

PRODUCER. Fi, can you...

ACTRESS. Sure. The second paragraph?

The ACTRESS *speaks in* LULLY*'s accent while more footage of the family and the Dignitas clinic plays. She is careful to time key words to time-coded bits of the film, the* EDITOR *semi-conducts her.*

Finding an end is one of life's deep conundrums. We all seek the elegant closure of a great novel or a magisterial symphony – the dying fall – but life is often more random, spiteful even. The lingering cancer, the twilight of dementia, the slow wasting of the faculties – there is no resolution here, merely painful white noise. This is not a clean page break to life's treasured narrative, but rather a meandering series of commas and hesitating, unfinished sentences. The pen misplaced, the...

PRODUCER. I mean, that's not how it would be, of course.

EXEC. She said all this?

PRODUCER. Well, it's from an article actually, but it's still her words. Or at least in translation – we know how alienating subtitles can be for British audiences.

EXEC. Hmm. Hmm.

PRODUCER. I mean, we'd make it more conversational. Or not? Maybe it works like that.

EXEC. I don't know how comfortable I feel about this, though. After all the recent fuss…

PRODUCER. No, I realise…

EXEC. I mean, we can't just cover our cuts like that any more.

EDITOR. It's not covering, just selecting. I mean, it's basic Eisenstein.

EXEC. Sure, I know that, but it could get us in shit with Ofcom.

Beat.

ACTOR. Eisenstein?

EXEC (*thinking while spooling through the script*). Hmm. Hmm.

EDITOR (*quietly to the* ACTOR). You show an old lady in a rocking chair, you cut to a man walking through the woods, then cut to a kettle boiling. Tension. We make up a story even if nothing links them at all.

EXEC (*absently*). The old 'active audience'.

ACTOR. Right.

EDITOR. This is it without the cutaway.

He runs the film which jumps abruptly to LULLY*'s tears.*

ACTRESS. That's just wrong.

EDITOR. It's what Watson would do; show the cut.

EXEC. You don't have any more footage of the boy himself, do you?

The EDITOR *keeps spooling back.*

PRODUCER. No. We don't. The mother became very emotional and started to attack the father, saying it was his idea and stuff, and then he really just shut down and... but we still feel we've got something really...

EDITOR....Really...

An anxious pause.

EXEC. It just... Look, here's the thing: (*Suddenly passionate.*) the thing is, I suppose, that at the moment we just don't seem to have anything, well, edgy enough. I mean, there's a great idea here, but without the family stuff, the access... you know, the McGuffin... we sort of just stand back. We need... we need some chaos, some energy, some pain! I mean, we have a fourteen-year-old boy here, willing to take his life... to end his life... because of this terrible, this terrible thing he –

PRODUCER. Sure.

EXEC. – and yet there's no real contact with him; I mean, I realise you've got the guys here and can try adding some re-enactment, but I'm still not sure we're really getting anywhere, or anywhere interesting. (*Beat.*) Look, J, MacDonald and Broomfield have got some really provocative stuff opening the series, I mean, you know that, of course, you know that, we wanted something more in the vein of *Shadows*.

PRODUCER. I know, I know.

EXEC. I mean, I know it's... you're probably fed up with hearing it, I mean, it's practically a fucking cliché after all, but that shot of... in *Shadows*, the famous one, when the Serbian soldier just cracked, I mean, he just wept, didn't he?

PRODUCER. He did. He wept.

EXEC. And you see, why am I telling you, I mean, you know all this, of course you do, but then – when he cried, we knew, we just *knew*, that he'd been there at the massacre. And the whole story, the entire thing, hinged on that one moment, just suddenly from nowhere, it was extraordinary...

PRODUCER. It was. I know.

EXEC. And there in one moment we had the whole story and, not only that, we had an ending – a fucking gold-plated, BAFTA-munching, fuck-you-too-Yentob ending!

PRODUCER. I know.

EXEC. Here we have a great ending, I mean, the kid is dead! I know, forgive me... But where's the coverage?

PRODUCER. I know.

EXEC. Look, J. J. I know you. I know you're not like the others.

PRODUCER. Thanks. I mean, which others?

EXEC. Greengrass. Loach. All those arseholes... Fucking off to drama as soon as they could. 'Auteurs.'

ACTRESS. I love Loach...

EXEC. Of course you do. You're an actor. But this is Factual and we do it a bit differently here, keep it real. The mirror up to nature, yes?

ACTRESS. I'm just saying that...

EXEC. Look, J, J, just keep, keep digging! I mean, just follow your hunch, your nose. We can't afford for this to be sterile... dull, to be frank. We've already spent a lot – a lot! – of money out here. Just remember, it's a series of personal films; secret histories, things you'd never find on your normal 'Sex and the Third Reich' channels – the cutting edge, yes?

PRODUCER. Sure.

EXEC (*quietly*). Look, I know you've got a lot invested in this, J – personally, I mean. It was your sister, wasn't it, who was ill for a long time?

PRODUCER. Yes.

EXEC. Yes. Well... I know it will come together if you just free it up a bit – make it matter more. It's all about access, remember.

PRODUCER. Of course.

EXEC. Anyway, I've got to be on a plane in a couple of hours, but I'll call when I'm back in the office and we can talk more. Okay?

PRODUCER. Sure.

EXEC. See where we're at, eh? Okay. Catch you guys later. It's great work.

He breezes out. Beat.

ACTOR. Access?

EDITOR. He's right. If we don't get more personal testimony we're fucked. We might as well have made a bloody docu-drama.

ACTRESS. I thought this was a docu-drama?

EDITOR. No, no, no, no. This is a drama-documentary.

Beat.

ACTOR. Sorry, what is the difference between a docu-drama and a drama-documentary?

EDITOR. A drama-doc is what we're doing – a documentary with some dramatic reconstructions, whereas a docu-drama is a scripted film of real-life events.

ACTRESS. Like *Bloody Sunday*.

EDITOR. Exactly.

ACTOR. So why aren't we just making this as a docu-drama? Lose the real-life stuff and just use reconstruction?

PRODUCER. Because we don't have the budget and because I still believe that real people have something, a texture, an authenticity...

ACTOR. Well, we can recreate that.

ACTRESS. But not tonight.

PRODUCER. No, we can't recreate it! The dramatised scenes give us narrative, but it's the real footage that provides the tone... the atmosphere... the emotion...

EDITOR. It can't be cosmetic – Sarah Lancashire staring into the middle distance, all that bollocks. Everyone goes on about wanting to be in drama, drives me mad.

ACTRESS. Do they?

EDITOR. It's all one big ladder. At the bottom is radio, but everyone in radio secretly wants to be up in telly. We're at the bottom of telly, docs and drama-docs, and above us is drama. But even there there's a ladder: docu-drama at the foot and then serials and then series and then on up to the dizzy heights of the one-off drama feature. But then, just when you get to the very top, you realise that all you really want to do is make movies. And though you started out wanting to use the camera as a window onto the real world, you end up as James fucking Cameron.

Beat.

PRODUCER. Well, thanks, Stu, but all I want is to make this fucking film.

ACTOR. So what's the problem then?

PRODUCER. Like he said. Access. Without access we're nowhere.

Beat.

EDITOR. What next then, boss?

PRODUCER. I'm not sure.

Silence. Then a knock at the door.

EDITOR. That'll be the pizzas. Come in!

Enter the FATHER. He is alternatively mellifluous and violent in his manner. Like the other characters who will follow him, there is something luminous, ethereal – 'other' – about him. His intensity is in stark contrast to the unfinished, low-energy sentences of the film-makers.

FATHER. Excuse me.

EDITOR. Sorry, can we help you?

FATHER (*comes forward a little*). As a matter of fact, you can. We have come here in search of an author.

EDITOR. Sorry, we're actually in the middle of an edit, perhaps you could try the site office?

FATHER. But it says here, on the door – *Storyville*?

EDITOR. That's just the name of the series.

FATHER. So you do not tell stories here?

PRODUCER (*absently, referring to the EXEC*). Not good ones, apparently.

FATHER. Quality is not an issue. We will provide that. Behold.

At the door, enter five others. The MOTHER is dressed in black and wears a thick widow's veil, her eyes downcast. The STEPDAUGHTER is dashing, almost impudent, beautiful. She wears mourning dress too. She is followed by the BOY (also dressed in black) and the GIRL. Lingering at the back of the group is the SON. He looks as if he has come against his will. This is recognisably the family who vanished from the Dignitas waiting room earlier.

The MOTHER falls, sobbing, to her knees, before calmly standing up again in a position of despair. The mime is almost kabuki-like in its precision. Beat.

FATHER. You see. Depth of feeling is not a problem here.

The room is uneasy.

EDITOR. Look, I'm sure the site office will be able to...

ACTOR (*quietly*). Do you want me to call security?

FATHER. As I say, all we require is an author.

EDITOR. An author? What author?

FATHER. Any author.

PRODUCER. There's no author here.

FATHER. No script?

PRODUCER. Yes, of course we've got a script, but...

FATHER. And who wrote your script?

PRODUCER. Well, I did, but it's not my words as such...

STEPDAUGHTER. Wonderful! We can be your new work.

ACTOR. Brilliant.

PRODUCER. This is a joke, right?

FATHER. No, what are you saying? We bring you a drama.

STEPDAUGHTER. We certainly do that!

EDITOR. Look, I'm sorry, you're obviously a bit confused. We're very busy here, so if you could just go back to the site office and tell them that you took a wrong turn by the catering truck. (*Mouths to the* ACTRESS.) Mad.

FATHER. You of all people must know that life is full of absurdities, coincidences... accidents... that have no need to appear real, since they are, in fact, true.

ACTOR. What's he talking about?

FATHER. Perhaps it is you who are mad? Insisting these stories, these dramas you are 'observing', are a kind of truth. But, if I may, selected highlights are a poor substitute for life itself...

EDITOR. Whatever. (*To the* ACTOR.) Yeah, call security…

FATHER. To make seem true that which isn't true, for the purposes of entertainment… Isn't that what you do here? Better surely to submit to the pure, unstructured energy of the creative imagination, where one may be born as almost anything – a tree, a stone, a butterfly; a character in a drama.

The ACTRESS *laughs and the* FATHER *winces.*

I'm sorry you laugh. We have all been born as characters.

We carry within us a tragedy.

EDITOR (*moving the* FATHER *towards the door*). Come on, get out!

FATHER (*resisting the* EDITOR). No, no, please…

The STEPDAUGHTER *advances towards the* PRODUCER, *smiling and coquettish.*

STEPDAUGHTER. Believe me, we really are six of the most fascinating characters; just abandoned ones.

FATHER. Yes, abandoned! Rejected by the author who created us, who was no longer willing or able to put us into a story. We have been discarded as an idea – perhaps too troubling to countenance. This was a real crime; because a character whose story has been told may laugh at death. He cannot die. To live for ever, who would not crave that? Immortality – through a writer who nourishes, who nurtures, unlike ours.

The PRODUCER *looks sceptical.*

We want to live!

ACTRESS. For ever?

FATHER. For a moment… through you. Our drama, our passion is within us, and we are impatient, no, we are desperate to play it!

STEPDAUGHTER. My passion! Ah, if you only knew! My passion for him!

She points to the FATHER *and mimes a sexual embrace.*
Then she breaks out into a loud laugh.

FATHER (*furiously*). Behave yourself! And don't laugh like
that! I can't bear it!

Suddenly the STEPDAUGHTER *sings and dances a punk-*
porn version of Cole Porter's 'My Heart Belongs to
Daddy'. The room agog – the FATHER *clenched in pain.*
She finishes.

STEPDAUGHTER. Film this story for us! You'll see the
moment when I... when this little angel here...

Takes the GIRL *by the hand and leads her to the*
PRODUCER.

Isn't she an angel? (*Kisses her.*) Well, when God suddenly
takes this dear little child away from her poor mother; and
this idiot here –

She seizes hold of the BOY *roughly and pushes him forward.*

– does the stupidest thing, like the fool he is, you will see me
run away. Yes, I shall be off. But the vanishing moment
hasn't come just yet. After all that went on between him and
me – our special relationship (*Indicating the* FATHER *with a*
horrible wink.) – I can't stay to see her (*Indicating the*
MOTHER.) desperate misery. Her whimpering for that
hateful creep... (*Indicating the* SON.) Look at him! See how
frigid he is, because he's the big man, the legitimate son. He
despises me, despises him, (*Pointing to the* BOY.) despises
this baby here; because... we are bastards. (*Goes to the*
MOTHER *and embraces her.*) And he doesn't want to recognise her as his mother – she who's the mother of us all. He
sneers at her as if she were only the mother to us three – bastards. Vicious little prig!

MOTHER. Stop it! For the sake of the children... (*She grows*
faint and is about to fall.) Oh God!

FATHER. Quick, a chair for the widow!

ACTRESS. Has she really fainted?

ACTOR. Just get her a chair!

The EDITOR *brings a chair, the others proffer assistance. The* MOTHER *tries to prevent the* FATHER *from lifting the veil which covers her face.*

FATHER. Look at her! Look at her!

MOTHER. No, no; stop it, please!

FATHER (*raising the* MOTHER*'s veil*). Let them see you!

MOTHER (*covering her face with her hands, in desperation*). Please don't let him persuade you! Just ignore him. Please!

PRODUCER. Is this woman your wife?

FATHER. Yes, my wife!

ACTRESS. But how can she be a widow then? If you are alive?

FATHER. Her story lies exactly in that paradox. She had a lover, a man who ought to be here.

MOTHER. No! No!

STEPDAUGHTER. He's dead. Luckily for him. A dead lover. We are in mourning for him, as you see.

FATHER. He isn't here, you understand, not because he is dead. He isn't here because (*Indicating the* MOTHER.) her story isn't the story of her love for two men, because she is incapable of feeling love, of feeling anything except possibly a little gratitude. She isn't a woman, she is a mother, and her tragedy lies in these four children she has had by two men.

MOTHER. I had them? Are you saying that I wanted them? It was his doing. It was him who pushed that other man on me, who forced me out.

STEPDAUGHTER. That's just not true.

MOTHER. Not true, isn't it?

STEPDAUGHTER. No, it isn't true. Liar.

MOTHER. And what can you possibly know about it?

STEPDAUGHTER. It isn't true. Don't believe it. (*To the* PRODUCER.) You want to know why she says so? For that fool there. (*Indicating the* SON.) She wants him to think that if she abandoned him when he was only two years old, it was because he (*Gestures at the* FATHER.) made her.

MOTHER. He forced me to it, on my children's life. (*To the* PRODUCER.) Ask him if it isn't true. Let him speak. (*To the* STEPDAUGHTER.) You don't know anything about it.

STEPDAUGHTER. I know you lived happily with my father while he was alive. Didn't you?

MOTHER. Yes, but…

STEPDAUGHTER. He loved you! (*To the* BOY, *angrily.*) It's true, isn't it? Tell them! Why don't you speak, you little shit?

MOTHER. Leave the poor boy alone. What are you trying to say? It's not my fault I was kicked out…

FATHER. It's true. It was my doing.

ACTRESS (*whispered to the* ACTOR). This is fucking ridiculous…

ACTOR. I know. So theatrical.

EDITOR. It's the last thing we need right now.

SON. Words! All these words…

FATHER. They're all that's left! I've tried everything else.

STEPDAUGHTER. Oh yes! You've tried everything else of course! Because before there were justifications, you tried to pay your way out of it all. The dirty bundle of notes from your sweaty pockets. Just for me!

SON. This is sick.

STEPDAUGHTER. Sick? There they were on the bedside table in the upstairs room of Mr Pace's shop. You know Pace – one of those men who attract poor little girls from nice families pretending they can do a little sewing, maybe some alterations for their clients, just so long as they do it in their underwear. (*Gesturing at the* FATHER.) And he thinks he has bought the right to lord it over all of us. Though of course in the end he got it all for free. And remembering the noise he made, I think he enjoyed the whole –

MOTHER. Where's your shame?!

STEPDAUGHTER. Shame! This is my revenge! I am dying to live that scene... The room... I see it... Here is the window, net curtains, there the divan, the soiled sheets, the mirror, the cash on the table, the red light. I see it. I see it. I can feel it... But maybe you shouldn't be looking now: I am almost naked after all, and only just thirteen, of course. But I'm not blushing, not sweating, not panting: I leave all that to him. (*Indicating the* FATHER.)

EDITOR. I'm lost now.

FATHER. It's understandable. I would ask you, all of you, to use your discretion here, and let me speak before you swallow her –

STEPDAUGHTER. Unfortunate word.

FATHER. – accusations. Let me put it this way...

STEPDAUGHTER. Ah yes, your own special way.

FATHER. She sees it one way, I another, he a third, but each from his own perspective – selective memory. For example: this woman takes my pity for her as an especially brutal form of cruelty.

MOTHER. You drove me out!

FATHER. You hear that? I drove her out! She really believes I sent her away.

MOTHER. You know how to talk, and I don't. It's the truth!
Believe me, after he had married me... God only knows
why... I was just ignored...

FATHER. For heaven's sake, I married you for that very
humility! I loved your simplicity.

The MOTHER *is about to contradict him.*

You see she denies it! She pours her love into the children
and shuts her mind to everything else.

ACTRESS (*to the* PRODUCER). Excuse me, but are we going
to be filming any more tonight? It's just, I've got a babysitter
waiting at the hotel and...

FATHER. Capture our story, I beg you!

ACTOR (*looking at the* STEPDAUGHTER). It is kind of
extraordinary...

ACTRESS. Well, I can see what you're interested in... J, can
we please call it a night? We've all been at it since five-thirty
and quite frankly I'm getting a little fed up.

PRODUCER. Is this leading anywhere?

STEPDAUGHTER. Just you wait!

PRODUCER. Okay.

The ACTRESS *groans.*

FATHER (*sitting*). I had taken on a secretary to help with the
family business. There was a lot to do, the paperwork was
mounting, so he came to live with us, to help with the
audit... A pleasant fellow, of poor education, but conscien-
tious. Things began to develop between this man and her.
(*Indicating the* MOTHER.) They got on very well. It was as
if they already knew one another. But there was nothing
sordid about it, you understand.

STEPDAUGHTER. All that comes later!

FATHER. I wanted them to be happy – and, yes, I wanted hap-
piness too. It had got to the point where I couldn't say a

word to either of them without their catching one another's
eye. Furtive little looks that began to drive me mad.

PRODUCER. And this is when you decided to send him away –
the secretary?

FATHER. Yes. But then I had to endure the spectacle of this
poor woman moping about the house, the family home, like
some stray animal you take in off the street.

MOTHER. Ah yes...

FATHER. Well, it's true, isn't it?

MOTHER. To banish me – and then to hold onto my son, my
child... How could you? To steal my baby from me, to deny
me access, for all those years!

FATHER. But not out of cruelty. I did it so that he should
grow up healthy and strong, living with his father in the
country.

STEPDAUGHTER. Yeah, just look how strong he is now.

FATHER. It is hardly my fault. I sent him to a good school, took
him hunting, played football with him. Tried to be a father
and a mother to him –

The STEPDAUGHTER *bursts into a noisy laugh.*

Oh, stop it! Stop it! I can't stand it.

PRODUCER (*to the* STEPDAUGHTER). Do you mind?

STEPDAUGHTER. But imagine! Family values... from him!

FATHER. Yes, I had needs, urges! Who doesn't? It's proof that I
am a man! You pounce on that as a contradiction, well, it is,
it's how you know I'm alive! I couldn't live with that woman
any longer. Not so much for the boredom she induced as for
the pity I felt for her.

MOTHER. And so he turned me out –

FATHER. – I provided for you! Yes, I sent her to that other
man... I gave her freedom – from me.

MOTHER. To free himself.

FATHER. Yes. I admit it. It was also a liberation for me. But with poisonous results. I meant well. I did it more for her sake than mine. It's the truth! (*To the* MOTHER.) And you were never out of my sight until he whisked you away to another town, like the jealous fool he was. Before then, I watched tenderly as their new family blossomed. She'll tell you. (*Points to the* STEPDAUGHTER.)

STEPDAUGHTER. Oh yes, that's true enough. When I was a child, not even in a proper bra, you know, with plaits over my shoulders and knickers longer than my skirts, I used to see him waiting outside the school for me to come out. He came to see how I was growing up.

FATHER. That is outrageous.

STEPDAUGHTER. No. Why?

FATHER. Completely outrageous. From the moment she left, the place seemed deserted. I was like a lost puppy alone in empty rooms. I had sent this boy here (*Indicating the* SON.) off to the finest boarding school in the country, but when he came back, he was like a stranger to me. With no mother to stand between us, he grew up a selfish, solitary figure, unconnected to me, emotionally, intellectually... It was curiosity at first, and then a genuine affection that drew me towards her new family, a family that in a way I had brought into the world. Thoughts of them slowly began to fill the lonely void within me. I wanted to know if she was happy, I suppose. I wanted to think of her as happy, away from me at last. And so, for the assurance that they were still all together as a family, I used to stand at the school gates at the end of the day and watch and wait for... that child.

STEPDAUGHTER. Yes, yes. That's certainly true. He used to follow me in the street and smile at me, wave his hand, like this – sometimes beckon me. I would look at him, wondering who he was, so I told my mother, who guessed at once. Then

she didn't want to send me to school for... well, a few days,
I think; and when I finally went back, there he was again –
looking so ridiculous – with a paper parcel in his hands. He
followed me on the train home and, although it wasn't that
crowded a carriage, he began to press close to me, rubbing at
my thighs and... well, when I got off he followed me down
the lane and then suddenly he went down on one knee, drew
out a pretty little dress from the parcel, and a bunch of
flowers – pansies, I think – all for me...

PRODUCER (*engrossed*). Then what?

SON (*contemptuously*). Fantasy! A complete fantasy!

STEPDAUGHTER. Exactly! A fantasy born of passion!

PRODUCER. So, nothing actually happened?

FATHER. This is only the introduction, the background. Life
has moved on and she, as you see, is no longer a schoolgirl
with plaits down her back...

STEPDAUGHTER. ...and knickers showing below her skirt...

FATHER. It all happened quite suddenly; he had got some new
job, and I couldn't find neither hide nor hair of them. And
so, inevitably, I think, they began to fade from my thoughts.
But the tragedy culminates when they come back. It's now
that the drama really begins; something new... complex,
disturbing.

STEPDAUGHTER. As soon as my father died...

FATHER. It was absolute misery for them. They came back but
I was never told. Because of her stupidity! (*Pointing to the*
MOTHER.) She can barely write her own name, but she
could have got her daughter to write to me, tell me that they
were in need...

MOTHER. And how was I to know he felt this way? All caring
and considerate? The father. You go on and on, but just
imagine being in my position. After so many years apart, and
all that had happened...

FATHER. Am I to be held responsible for his carrying you off? It is on their return, when I am impelled by my miserable flesh... Ah! The desperation of a man on his own... Not old enough to do without women, and not young enough to go and look for one without making a fool of himself in some awful bar or sordid hotel. The misery of it, the horror. Well, just go without, you say? Yes, yes. I know. Outwardly, we are clothed in a certain dignity. But every man knows the secret thoughts, the unspeakable things that are damned within the privacy of the heart. On one's own, one gives way to temptation, only to rise from it again, afterwards, eager to wash it away, pretend it never happened... All men know those feelings. Even if not all have the courage to admit it.

STEPDAUGHTER. They still all do it, though.

FATHER. Yes, but in secret. It takes courage to admit it, to confess. A man who comes clean about his bestial desires is, to my mind, better than a man who refuses to recognise the darkness within. A girl, on the other hand, will bead you with her dirty little eyes until you can't help but seize her. And no sooner does she feel herself in your grasp than she closes them again. It's the sign that her mission has been accomplished, the sign by which she says to the man: 'Blind yourself, for I am blind.'

STEPDAUGHTER. Yes, well, sometimes there comes a point when she just can't close them any more! Because all she can see in front of her is the grubby little dribbler with his eyes clamped onto her unformed chest. Urghh! I'm sorry, but this whole thing makes me sick – all this justification, I can't stand it! When a man seeks to 'simplify' life, throwing aside every semblance of feeling, all sense of duty, modesty, shame... then nothing is more vomit-inducing than a certain kind of remorse – crocodile tears, that's what it is. Let's just do it, for heaven's sake. Enough of this wretched analysis, let's just get on with it.

She starts to take off her clothes and shoes.

EDITOR. Do we need to see all this?

FATHER. Yes, we do! To put things in context. In order that they might, perhaps, be understood. Look, I couldn't possibly know that after the death of my secretary, they had returned to our hometown, that they were living in poverty, and that she (*Pointing to the* MOTHER.) had gone to work for this man Pace.

STEPDAUGHTER. A really posh outfit. Nice window display, hats made to order, lace, all that. But upstairs...

MOTHER. I knew nothing about all that – what went on upstairs. We, who had had everything, were now poor immigrants, even if it was our hometown we had been so long away. Mr Pace was kind and supportive, he gave me work sewing the lining into his hats. It never entered my mind that he offered me work because he had his eye on my daughter.

STEPDAUGHTER. Poor Mummy! Do you know what that man did when I brought him back the work my mother had finished at home? He would point out to me that I had torn the lining, and it was me that had to pay for it. While this poor creature here believed she was sacrificing herself for me and these two children, sitting up all night sewing Mr Pace's hats... all the while I was busy in the upstairs room...

PRODUCER. And is this where you met...

STEPDAUGHTER. Him, him. Yes, an old client. This is what it's all been building to. The climax!

FATHER. She turned up. The mother turned up...

STEPDAUGHTER (*treacherously*). Almost in time!

FATHER. No, in time! Wasn't it in time? I'm sure I recognised her... in time. (*Beat.*) Well, after that, I took them back home with me... to my house. But this thing had happened...

STEPDAUGHTER. Not something natural, even between consenting adults.

FATHER. Alright! They can see the position we were in...

STEPDAUGHTER. But I wonder if they can – I mean, the exact position?

FATHER (*violently*). I mean, when we came home.

STEPDAUGHTER. That's right, 'Daddy', show your true colours!

FATHER. I'm not your father. When we got home... she, as you see her, and I unable to look her in the face... well, you can imagine...

STEPDAUGHTER. It was a joke! He wanted to bring me up from now on as a respectable young lady. Sensible clothes and nice manners. Just to make him feel better about himself. But what's done cannot be undone. Nor was it.

Pause.

FATHER. This is the essence of the tragedy! In a moment such as this, at the crux of our story, we are all suspended in time and space – branded by a single act. (*Beat.*) But you can't judge me by one terrible moment. Now you see the cruelty of this girl? She surprised me in a place where she ought not to have known me, just as I should never have existed for her; and she's trying to nail me to it, crucify me for it, for ever. And of course, we have to consider the others... him... (*Indicating the* SON.)

SON. Hey, leave me out of this! I'm nothing to do with any of this.

FATHER. What? You're not involved?

SON. I've got nothing to do with it, and I don't want to have; because you know well enough I wasn't made to be mixed up in all this with the rest of you.

STEPDAUGHTER. We're only common scum! He's the posh boy. If you've seen me giving him dirty looks, it's deliberate – because he knows how he's hurt me.

SON. Me?

STEPDAUGHTER. You! You! Did you or did you not deny us any semblance of hospitality when we arrived on your doorstep? Not so much as a 'How are you?' or 'Can I help you with anything?', or even just a friendly smile.

SON. It's easy for them to paint me as the villain of the piece. But can you imagine how I felt? A son, minding his own business in his own home, when one day I see turn up on my doorstep a cocky little slut asking for my father. And me knowing nothing of what had gone on between them. So then I see her come back the next day with that child and furtively take my father into the front room. And then I see her demanding money from him because he owes it to them!

FATHER. But I do owe it to them. I owe it to your mother.

SON. But how did I know? When had I ever seen or heard of her? One day she turns up and you say, 'This is your mother.' Can you imagine what was going on in my head? I don't want to say what I feel, what I felt. Even to myself. So count me out of this whole thing! Believe me, I am an 'unrealised' character, dramatically speaking; and I just don't fit in with them. Count me out. I can't speak. I'm mute. I refuse. Cut!

FATHER. Oh, you are so…

SON. How do you know what I'm like? When have you ever cared anything for me!

FATHER. He's right. I admit it. I admit it. But isn't that a story in itself? This aloofness of yours, so cruel to me and to your mother, who returns home and sees you almost for the first time grown up, who doesn't recognise you, but knows you are her son… (*Pointing out the* MOTHER *to the* PRO-DUCER.) See, she's crying!

STEPDAUGHTER. Like a fool!

FATHER. He says he doesn't come into the affair, but actually he is the heart of it. Look at that boy, always clinging to his mother, frightened and humiliated. Perhaps his situation is the most painful of all. Cut off, isolated. Because of this arrogant fool! He's made these poor children feel humiliated at being brought into someone else's home out of nothing more than begrudging charity. They are the blank image of their father – speechless, mysterious.

PRODUCER. We wouldn't focus on the children...

EDITOR. ...it's been a legal minefield.

FATHER. Don't worry, they'll disappear soon enough. In fact, the girl is the first to go. It's complicated. Look, we each clutch at our own version, but until you give us life then nothing can fully come out – in short, none of it can happen without you. Please. Help us.

Silence.

PRODUCER. Okay, look. What are you proposing?... I'm a film-maker, not a therapist.

STEPDAUGHTER (*stepping forward*). Then I'm ready for my close-up!

FATHER. Be quiet! Will we have our story told?

PRODUCER. Maybe we can do something for you.

EDITOR. What?!

PRODUCER (*to the* EDITOR). You saw the forecast, the weather isn't going to clear until tomorrow. We've got all the equipment, we could shoot here.

EDITOR. Here?

FATHER. You'll understand, we are born performers...

PRODUCER. You're not actors?

FATHER. We're born to perform...

ACTOR. They are – they're actors...

FATHER. No, no. We are in search of an author to flesh out our lives, and you must be that author.

PRODUCER. Me?

FATHER. Yes, you, you! Why not?

PRODUCER. I'm not a writer, we're a film-making collective…

FATHER. Realise us. Bring us to life.

Beat.

PRODUCER (*with new and impressive energy*). Okay. Somebody call the hotel. I need Flor, Danny… everyone.

ACTRESS. What??

PRODUCER. Get those lights rigged up. Peter, dig out the flats we used for the clinic.

EDITOR. There's just not enough room in here…

PRODUCER. We'll manage. We'll reconvene in twenty minutes.

EDITOR. But…

PRODUCER. Just do it, Stuart.

Lights snap. On the screens above we see an almost still shot of the Dignitas clinic in the snow. The PRODUCER, *the* ACTORS *and the* FAMILY *leave. The* CAMERAMAN *and the* RUNNER *enter. They start to assemble a set in the office. The* EDITOR *spools through material to be discarded. He watches some footage of the* PRODUCER *talking to camera while in the back seat of a car in Denmark.*

PRODUCER (*on-screen*). It's just so strange to finally be here… I should be feeling elated that Andrew's suffering is coming to an end, but actually, you know what? I feel an eerie sort of dread. I mean, I know Andrew is still committed one hundred per cent to going through with… it; and his parents seem just as sure, but for me I feel like we're hurtling towards something premature or dangerous or, I don't know, just out of our control. (*Beat*). Maybe it's the landscape here, or at least what we can see of it through all this bloody fog… (*Laughs.*) But all the issues that seemed so transparent before we left England just seem… murkier here.

Look, I never expected a harp and a holy choir, but I just hoped that the clinic might be somewhere a bit less desolate. I mean, look! (*Camera pans to window.*) There's just no one here at all, it's the loneliest place in the world. And somehow that makes everything that seemed clear seem, well, cloudy... It makes me think of...

She trails off. A long moment.

EDITOR (*off-screen*). J, we're still rolling...

The screen crackles into static. The EDITOR *continues to scan through material. He stops as a bearded man in a dog collar appears on the monitor. He peers towards the camera.*

Philip Ratcliffe, Bishop of Ely. Take four.

PRODUCER (*off-screen*). Thanks, Philip, if you could begin that again for me, please?

BISHOP. Of course... (*Coughs.*)

PRODUCER (*off-screen*). Just take your time.

BISHOP. Thanks... (*Coughs.*) Death is an absolute. It's the ending to the mortal experience and the moment we leave this earth to begin our life with God. So... Death belongs to God just as completely as life does. Death is sacred.

PRODUCER (*off-screen*). That argument, though, has little impact on those who don't share your views on faith...

BISHOP. No, I appreciate that. (*Beat.*) Look, I'm not interested in needless suffering, I don't seek to prolong pain. But I think everyone can understand that humanity doesn't... shouldn't... seek to control everything.

PRODUCER (*off-screen*). Can you explain what you mean?

BISHOP. I believe that to allow people to choose death, to impose it, before the natural time... is a hubristic and dangerous precedent. Our fate is not entirely in our own hands, thankfully! Whatever you call the force that is beyond ourselves... however you characterise that... it is undeniable that it exists and that it controls aspects of our existence. Including when we begin and when we end. And that, I find reassuring. Our creator, our author... these things are in his control.

The EDITOR *spools forward the tape. He stops as the camera settles on* ANDREW'S MOTHER *and* FATHER. *They sit in the Dignitas waiting room facing the camera.* ANDREW'S MOTHER *begins to shake with sobs. The camera stays on them as* ANDREW'S FATHER *reaches across to comfort her. She shakes him off violently. The camera stays on them for longer than is comfortable as she sobs and he stares implacably forward. The screen fills with static. The* EDITOR *stops the tape. He watches the set assembly continue.*

End of Act One.

ACT TWO

The EDITOR, *the* CAMERAMAN *and the* RUNNER *have set up some lights, a sound desk and two cameras. They are pointing at the set, which, despite its flimsiness, is recognisable as the Dignitas medical room. The* ACTOR *is sat on one of several folding chairs, reading the* Guardian. *The* ACTRESS *moves over to him.*

ACTRESS. Listen, did you speak to your agent?

ACTOR. I tried but it's too late. They've all gone. You?

ACTRESS. I just rang her at home. She said it's all in the contract. Any changes J wants to make, we have to...

She's interrupted by the bustling arrival of the PRODUCER, *who leads the* FATHER *and the rest of the* CHARACTERS. *She gestures to a row of six more folding chairs being laid out by the* RUNNER.

PRODUCER. Sir, if you and your family would like to take a seat, I'll be with you in a moment. Thank you. (*To the* CREW; *fast, efficient.*) Okay, are we here? I know it's late, but the sooner we start, the sooner we finish. (*Gestures to the set.*) We need to set up the interior of the room above Pace's shop? Stu?

EDITOR. What does that look like?

PRODUCER. I'm not sure yet, a bit like a bedsit, I suppose. A mattress, net curtains, you know the sort of thing. Can you check what we've got in store?

The EDITOR *goes off.*

(*To the* RUNNER.) Danny, can we distress the walls a bit? Nothing too blatant. Then we should be able to use these flats and the floor'll be fine.

RUNNER. Wicked.

PRODUCER (*to the* CAMERAMAN). Flor, I think it needs something… you remember that bleary quality from *Borstal Kids*?

CAMERAMAN. Not quite monochrome, but we can bleach-bypass it in after-effects?

PRODUCER. Exactly. Mostly fairly static, then maybe some POV once they start. Okay?

CAMERAMAN. Got it.

The EDITOR *sticks his head round the door.*

EDITOR. J, we've got the mattress and bedside table we used for the interior of Andrew's bedroom at the clinic?

PRODUCER. Great, let's use those. (*To the* STEPDAUGHTER, *gently.*) Excuse me, we're going to set up the room above Pace's shop. We've got a blue mattress and a bedside table, is there anything else you'd like us to try and find? Anything that would help to make it feel authentic?

STEPDAUGHTER. No, no! Blue won't do. The mattress was white, with a filthy grey sheet – dirty, but very large and *very* comfortable!

Beat.

EDITOR. We've only got the one.

PRODUCER. I'm not sure the colour actually matters.

STEPDAUGHTER. Doesn't matter?!

PRODUCER. I'm sorry, resources are limited, but we are going to try and make it feel accurate. Danny, get one of the grey blankets we used on the ward and we'll cover the mattress.

The RUNNER *has hung a tatty net curtain to the window and now goes to get the blanket. The* EDITOR *carries the mattress through.*

FATHER. And a mirror. A full-length mirror.

STEPDAUGHTER. Yes! We need a mirror to watch ourselves in, or how on earth will we manage?

RUNNER. The one from the office?

PRODUCER. Thanks, Danny. Now, if you'll bear with me for a moment longer, we're nearly ready to begin.

FATHER. Of course. And thank you.

The FATHER *and the rest of the* CHARACTERS *sit on the chairs. He watches the* PRODUCER.

PRODUCER. It's my pleasure. (*Moves over to the* ACTOR *and the* ACTRESS.) Guys, I know this seems weird, but... you know what I'm like... you get a hunch about these things. I think it's worth looking at.

ACTRESS. J, is this to do with what Bob said about Dignitas?

ACTOR. Because, you know, he's a prick.

PRODUCER. It's not that. Not just that. But, you know... he's right. Without access to the family, the film's going nowhere.

ACTOR. Andrew's father might still talk to us.

PRODUCER. He might. But in the meantime I can't afford to wait.

ACTRESS. This thing about them being characters...

ACTOR. They're either mad or they're better actors than we are.

PRODUCER. Maybe, but if something happened to them all, some event, some kind of appalling trauma, then maybe it's possible. Group delusions have happened before within family units.

ACTRESS. Well...

They look over at the CHARACTERS. *The* STEP-DAUGHTER *is tapping her foot anxiously; the* MOTHER *takes deep, heaving breaths behind her veil; the* SON *contemptuously turned away. And the* FATHER, *patiently watching. He smiles over at them.*

ACTOR. I think it's interesting, Fi…

PRODUCER. Worth a try, at least.

ACTRESS. Okay.

PRODUCER. Okay?

ACTRESS. Let's have a go.

PRODUCER. Right, the same format as before, a bit of recon-struction with you guys, and we'll cut it together with their talking heads. I'll ask them to take me through what hap-pened first, then you can come in and play them. Okay?

ACTRESS. No impro?

PRODUCER. Let's see what they give us first and then we can augment it with whatever we need. Peter?

ACTOR. I'm worried about the voice.

PRODUCER. I know…

ACTOR. It's just some of his phrasing is so weird. I'm not sure if I copy it accurately it's going to be credible.

PRODUCER. For now, just do your best – I wouldn't mind at all if you toned him down a little.

The ACTOR *nods.*

Thank you. (*To the* CHARACTERS.) Now, ladies and gen-tlemen, we're going to do our best to tell your story, if you're ready. It would be wonderful if you could walk us through what happened. The scene in the bedroom.

FATHER. I'm sorry, what do you mean, 'walk through it'?

PRODUCER. If you wouldn't mind, what would be ideal is if you could all show us exactly what happened… then the actors will know what to do when we come to shoot it.

FATHER. Excuse me, 'the actors will know'?

PRODUCER. In the filmed reconstruction of the scene, they'll be performing your roles.

FATHER. But we are the characters! We are the real thing.

PRODUCER (*glancing at the* ACTOR). Of course you are and it's wonderful that we have you here to tell your story. But I want to illustrate your first-hand testimony – which was so moving – with reconstructed scenes. And in those moments, you can't play yourselves. In order for the audience to be clear what is reconstruction, these actors will play you.

FATHER. With due respect. This man and woman will 'play' at being us, they will 'act' us. But they won't 'be' us. They'll want to be, pretend to be, but that isn't the same at all, is it? Given that you are fortunate enough to have us alive, able and willing before you, wouldn't it be better to film us in the scene, living and experiencing the moment ourselves?

PRODUCER. Sorry, I'm not explaining this very well. I do want you in the film, all of you. You'll be yourself, in the 'to camera' sections, when I'll interview you about how you feel and what exactly you did. But you can't act in the reconstructions. That's not the way docu-drama works.

FATHER. Let's change how it works! The genre clearly has limitations, but we will transcend them.

STEPDAUGHTER. Let me play myself! I promise you won't be disappointed!

PRODUCER. The reason I know it won't work is that I've tried it before. People playing themselves can't relax in front of the camera. Once they are observed, they lose their authenticity, become self-conscious, fake. As soon as they're on camera, they begin to lie. I know it seems perverse, but actually these performers will look and sound more real than you do.

ACTOR. I can assure you that we'll be sensitive in the way we portray you and your family.

Pause.

EDITOR (*to the* CHARACTERS). It's like in *United 93*, the 9/11 film? Some of those air-traffic controllers were the real guys and it was weird. They just stood out.

PRODUCER. Our audience isn't stupid, they know they're watching actors, but they trust us to tell the truth.

FATHER. A trust based on what?

PRODUCER. On twenty years of this kind of work. These actors, with me directing them, are so relaxed in front of a camera that you'd swear they didn't know they were being watched.

FATHER. Their performances are more real than the people they are portraying?

PRODUCER. In a way, yes, because they don't edit themselves. They don't shy away from confronting the truth, whatever that might be.

FATHER. I think I begin to understand.

PRODUCER. Peter has worked with me for years and he'll be playing you. (*Indicating the* FATHER.) Fiona here will attempt to do justice to you. (*Indicating the* STEP-DAUGHTER.)

STEPDAUGHTER. That woman there? (*Bursts out laughing.*)

ACTRESS. Is there a problem?

The STEPDAUGHTER *is rocking with laughter.*

FATHER. Oh dear.

PRODUCER. What's the matter?

STEPDAUGHTER. There is no way that she can play me!

ACTRESS. What?

STEPDAUGHTER. Look at her! Look at me!

ACTRESS. Well, why not?

STEPDAUGHTER. Look at her!

ACTRESS. Oh, for God's sake, J, this is just insulting...

STEPDAUGHTER (*doubled up with laughter*). No, no, excuse me...

PRODUCER. Fi, I'm sorry, hang on. (*To the* STEP-DAUGHTER.) Do you mind?

ACTOR. We don't have to take this...

STEPDAUGHTER (*trying to pull herself together*). I wasn't laughing at her! I was laughing at myself – I just can't see any resemblance, that's all! I'm sure you're very good... but you... you aren't in the least like me –

FATHER (*stepping in*). She's right, you know. That's the problem with your impersonations. How can you get close to us? Our essential selves. Our souls. How can you offer anything more than a shadow of the original?

PRODUCER. My films, if they work at all, work as an... enhancement of the original story. Our reconstructions will present the events, free of emotion, in order that the audience can understand the essence of what happened, the bare bones of the narrative. The two strands, testimony and reconstruction, work alongside each other. And together, they offer the viewer 'more than truth'.

ACTOR. Perhaps you saw the mountaineering film, *Touching the Void*?

FATHER. The void? (*Beat.*) You must understand, we who exist only as we are, we suffer terribly to see anyone 'playing' at being us...

EDITOR (*starting to lose patience*). Oh, for Christ's sake...

PRODUCER. Stu, please. A bit of respect.

EDITOR. I'm sorry. (*Beat.*) You asked me to tell you when it was two o'clock.

PRODUCER. Okay, listen... I can understand your wanting to protect yourselves... but what we're doing here, what you've asked me to do for you, it's going to take courage from everyone. This is an expensive experiment and if it fails it'll be an expensive failure. (*Beat*.) We've stopped work on a documentary about a special hospice in town where they offer assisted suicide to the terminally ill. We've lived with the patients and doctors for nearly six months. We feel an acute obligation to them. But we've stopped work in order to help you and your family and I can give you no greater guarantee of our seriousness than that.

FATHER (*smiling*). Please excuse me. We have no desire to hold things up. Pray, continue.

PRODUCER. Thank you. Danny, are we ready?

The RUNNER *appears from behind the set.*

RUNNER. Yup, all done.

PRODUCER. What do you think? Does that look like the shop?

STEPDAUGHTER. I don't recognise it at all.

PRODUCER. We're not going to be able to reconstruct the place exactly, it's meant to be representative... it stands for all the rooms in which women have to do what you did. What would help it?

STEPDAUGHTER. Well, for a start, the money. A great heap of it there, on the bedside table.

PRODUCER. That's great. These are the details that'll make all the difference. Stu, get some cash for the table, please. (*Quietly, intimately to the* STEPDAUGHTER.) I know this is difficult, but if you could take us through it, slowly, as it happened.

STEPDAUGHTER. Oh, I'm going to take you through it. Every second of it.

PRODUCER. You are alone in the room?

STEPDAUGHTER. Oh no, Pace is with me.

Beat.

PRODUCER (*to the* FATHER). Do we have any way of contacting Pace? With your permission, I'd love to hear from him.

FATHER. He isn't with us. But we may be able to call him...

PRODUCER. Great, if you have a number, that would be...

FATHER. One moment. Sir, do you have, in your store, any ladies' hats?

ACTOR. Hats?

RUNNER. We've got loads.

FATHER. Could you bring a selection through here, please?

PRODUCER. Why do you need hats? We don't need to film the shop, just the room upstairs...

FATHER. To summon Mr Pace! He makes his living making and selling beautiful hats. By displaying the articles of his trade we may just persuade him to appear.

ACTOR. I thought he was a pimp?

The RUNNER *comes back in carrying an armful of hats.*

FATHER. Ah, lay them here on the mattress... that's right.

He does so. Pause.

PRODUCER. Now what?

FATHER. Now we wait.

Silence. All wait, staring at the set. The CAMERAMAN *quietly finishes making adjustments to the camera and begins to film the empty room. The image appears on monitors and screens around the studio. He zooms in on the mattress and then the blanket, which suddenly twitches. Everyone jumps.*

STEPDAUGHTER. Oh God, there he is! There he is!

A hand appears from under the blanket, followed by an arm, a body and then the face of PACE, *a rodenty, furtive man who looks like what he is.*

FATHER. It's him! I said so, didn't I? There he is!

He moves forward and shakes PACE*'s hand, respectfully.*

Sir! Thank you for joining us.

PRODUCER. How did you do that?

EDITOR. Fucking hell...

The STEPDAUGHTER *runs onto the set and is embraced by* PACE. *The* FATHER *steps back as* PACE *kisses her on the lips, pulling her head back hard by her hair to do so. She wraps her arms around him as he begins to lick her face aggressively. She yowls and barks like a dog. His hands are up her skirt.*

PRODUCER. That is... Where did he come from?

EDITOR. It's a trick. He must've sneaked round whilst we were talking.

PRODUCER. How did he get in here in the first place?

FATHER (*smiling*). Why are you so ready to doubt the power of the imagination? Who is to impersonate Mr Pace in your film? Well, here is Mr Pace himself, what could be more real than that? You see, she recognised him and went to him at once. Now you're going to witness the scene! Indeed, it appears to have already begun...

The STEPDAUGHTER *and* PACE *are whispering to each other.*

PRODUCER. Hang on, hang on, Stu, Flor.

She gestures to the crew, who start to film the scene. It's very peculiar, with strange, stylised gestures repeated – the kiss, the slap, the running away, the pull back – with a soundtrack of whispered words, grunts and squeals. The FATHER *watches to one side, sadly.*

CAMERAMAN. Er, J, I'm not getting that at all...

EDITOR. What are they doing?

ACTRESS. I can't hear them.

ACTOR. We can't understand what they're saying.

PRODUCER. Okay, *cut*! (*Walking up onto set*.) I'm sorry, but I have to ask you to be a little louder.

STEPDAUGHTER. Louder? What are you talking about? These things can't be shouted out. If I have talked about them before, it was only to humiliate him. (*Gestures at the* FATHER.) But with Mr Pace, it's quite a different matter.

PRODUCER (*to the* RUNNER). Danny, can you get her a radio mic? (*To the* STEPDAUGHTER.) I think what you're doing is fantastic, I just really want to hear the dialogue.

The RUNNER *grabs a radio mic and attaches it to the* STEPDAUGHTER. *She runs over to the sound desk*.

RUNNER. Yup... Just speak into it for me, please... One-two-three-four...

STEPDAUGHTER. One-two-three-four...

Her voice echoes around the room.

PRODUCER. Okay, thanks. Can we go again, please?

The STEPDAUGHTER *is hiding her face*.

What's the matter?

FATHER. She's embarrassed. She knows that in a matter of minutes I'll be behind the door, listening... In fact, I'm a fool to put it off any longer, I should be there now, awaiting my shame.

He goes and stands behind the door.

PRODUCER. Hang on, hang on! We can't just plough on.

STEPDAUGHTER. No, get on with it at once! I'm just dying to act this bit.

PRODUCER. But first, we have to understand the scene between you and this man...

STEPDAUGHTER. For goodness' sake! It's quite simple, he's telling me what you know already: that Mamma's work is badly done again; that I must be a good girl and do as I'm told to help the family.

PACE (*suddenly, in a thick, smokey accent*). I'm just being a friend to the girl. Her best friend in the world.

Beat.

ACTOR. God, is that how he speaks?

PRODUCER. Peter, please...

ACTOR. And why is he dressed like that? I thought this was meant to be authentic... it's just indulgent...

PACE (*stepping forward*). Hey, friend. It's not polite to talk about someone like that when they're in the room. And it's incredibly fucking stupid to talk about me like that any-fucking-time.

PRODUCER (*finally snapping*). Peter, *please*, can we just get on? Tonight, we're trying this. Tomorrow, we'll see. I just need footage... any tonal problems we can fix later. (*Beat.*) We've got enough, I think it's obvious what the conversation between you two will be about.

STEPDAUGHTER. Yes, it's obvious! He tells me to spend the evening with a 'fine old gentleman', someone who'll be nice to me, take care of me. An old gentleman who'll be gentle with me...

PACE. He's not so old, love. And not as sick as some of them. There won't be any of that stuff from last week, alright? None of the –

MOTHER (*lunging for him*). You bastard!

STEPDAUGHTER. Mummy, don't!

FATHER (*restraining the* MOTHER). Please be calm, don't get excited! Sit down now! (*To the* PRODUCER, *apologetically.*) They can't be in a room together. That's why we didn't bring him with us to begin with. He can't open his mouth without smut pouring out. Filthy, filthy words.

PRODUCER. Look, I think we've got a sense of it... let's move on.

STEPDAUGHTER. Hysterics? Oh, just you wait. Go on then, leave me to it, leave me to the old gentleman.

PACE. Have fun, sweetheart. And do as you're told.

And quick as a flash, PACE exits through the door of the set. The STEPDAUGHTER and the FATHER see each other for a moment through the doorway, before PACE slams it shut behind him and walks around the back of the flats. The crew wait for him to appear at the other side. Eventually, the EDITOR walks round to look for him.

EDITOR. Yeah, he's gone.

ACTRESS. This is really creepy.

ACTOR. J?

STEPDAUGHTER (*shouting to the FATHER*). Now, your entrance. Don't bother with the door, let's suppose you've already come in.

Slowly, the FATHER steps into the room.

Stand there, yes! I'm here with bowed head, feigning modesty. Come on! Say it! Say, 'Good morning, Miss,' in that peculiar tone, that special tone...

PRODUCER (*to the FATHER, as he steps onto the set*). How did you feel as you made your way to Pace's shop?

FATHER. I felt the way I... the way I always felt.

PRODUCER. Can you describe that?

FATHER (*very halting, strained*). A kind of numbness... inevitability. I moved like someone sleepwalking, from my house, into the town. And then I stood outside the shop... for hours. I can't remember a single thought I had in that time.

When one reaches my age, one learns to separate the head and the heart from the desire. My head, I had switched off... my heart, I chose to ignore... but my desire prompted me and I obeyed, as it guided me back to that spot, outside the shop... and often guided me in.

PRODUCER. How often?

FATHER. I beg your pardon?

PRODUCER. How often did you go there?

FATHER. I have no idea. Every time felt like the first. But each time he welcomed me back like an old friend and I knew I'd been there before.

PRODUCER (*nodding*). Okay. Standby. Father and Stepdaughter, rehearsal take one, action.

The FATHER *and the* STEPDAUGHTER *begin to play the scene. It has a heightened quality, like watching a play in translation. Every gesture is slow, specific, carrying meaning.*

FATHER. Good afternoon.

STEPDAUGHTER. Good afternoon!

FATHER. Ah... but... forgive me, this isn't the first time that you've done this?

STEPDAUGHTER. No, sir.

FATHER. Ah good. More than once? (*Waits for her to answer, then:*) Well then, there's no need to be so shy, is there? May I take off your hat?

STEPDAUGHTER. No, sir... I'll do it myself.

And she begins a slow striptease. The MOTHER *watches the progress of the scene with varying expressions of sorrow, indignation, anxiety and horror. From time to time she sobs.*

MOTHER. Oh, my God, my God!

FATHER. Give it to me! I'll put it down.

He takes the hat from the STEPDAUGHTER*'s hands.*

But a dear little head like yours ought to have a smarter hat. Come and help me choose one from the stock, won't you?

STEPDAUGHTER. No, thank you, sir.

FATHER. Oh, come now. Don't talk like that. You must take it. I shall be upset if you don't. There are some lovely little hats here; and then Mr Pace will be pleased. He expects it, you know.

STEPDAUGHTER. No, no! I couldn't wear it!

FATHER. Oh, you're thinking about what they'd say at home if they saw you come in with a new hat? My dear girl, there's always a way round these little matters, you know.

STEPDAUGHTER. No, it's not that – I couldn't wear it because I am... as you see... you might have noticed... (*Showing her black dress.*)

FATHER. – in mourning! Of course: I beg your pardon: I'm frightfully sorry...

STEPDAUGHTER. No, I must thank you. There's no need for you to feel mortified or sorry. Don't think any more of what I've said. I must forget that I am dressed so...

PRODUCER. And... cut! (*To the* FATHER *and the* STEP-DAUGHTER.) Thank you, that was really very good. Thank you. (*To the* ACTORS.) It's fascinating, that, isn't it, where he offers her the hat?

STEPDAUGHTER. The best bit's coming now. Why can't we go on?

PRODUCER. Just a minute, please! (*To the* ACTORS.) Of course, it needs a bit more, you know...

ACTOR. Dirt?

ACTRESS. Exactly. They both know what's about to happen.

PRODUCER. Don't be afraid of the reality of it. Try and give me the primal essence of what's happening here. And remember, the room is filthy, it stinks of sex.

The ACTRESS *moves onto the set and takes the hat off the* STEPDAUGHTER's *head.*

STEPDAUGHTER. Hey!

ACTRESS. J, can we get something a little less cutsie, it feels a bit obvious. (*Picks up a different hat.*) What about that?

PRODUCER. Yeah, good! So you're there, your head bowed. (*To the* CAMERAMAN.) Flor, standby for a take, please. (*To the* FATHER *and the* STEPDAUGHTER.) Would you mind just stepping off the platform for a moment? Thank you.

The RUNNER *ushers a confused* FATHER *and* STEP-DAUGHTER *to one side.*

STEPDAUGHTER. But she isn't dressed in black.

PRODUCER. Quiet please. Just for a moment. *And… action!*

The door opens, and the ACTOR *enters. The scene as played by the* ACTORS *is a different thing, though it's in no way a parody. It's ultra-naturalistic, like a Ken Loach film, all hesitation and unfinished sentences.*

ACTOR. Erm – (*Coughs.*) Good after… er, Miss…

ACTRESS. Good afternoon.

Long pause.

ACTOR. This isn't the first time, is it?

PRODUCER. Good, but not quite so heavy. Again.

Long pause.

ACTOR. This isn't the first time, is it?

ACTRESS. No. (*Pause.*) No.

ACTOR. You've been here before, more than once.

Silence.

PRODUCER. And the slow nod.

ACTOR. There's no need to be shy…

FATHER. Oh! No, no!

PRODUCER. Cut! Sir, I'm sorry, but you must keep quiet. That take is ruined. We'll have to go again from the top.

STEPDAUGHTER. If anyone said 'Good afternoon' to me like that, I'd burst out laughing.

FATHER. Yes, yes, the manner, the tone…

PRODUCER (*exasperated*). We're trying to tell your story, which I thought was what you wanted. You have to let us do it our way!

FATHER. We want to assist you, believe me! We can't help it… when they act like that, skilled as they undoubtedly are, they cannot get close to us.

ACTOR. What do you mean, 'act like that'? That's naturalism!

FATHER. But it isn't natural at all! Not to us. What you have is yours, it could never be ours.

PRODUCER (*to the* ACTORS). Maybe this is just a waste of time…

FATHER. There is no better way to spend time! You look at me as if I was insane.

PRODUCER (*getting really frustrated now*). No, of course not, you're not insane! You are just a character whose author has abandoned him! But unless an author appears to prove your story, how can we be expected to believe you?

FATHER (*louder, more commanding*). Look at us and listen to us. Do not interpret, do not reconstruct. You ask for proof? We are no more than what we are. Utterly, irreducibly ourselves. Not by being entirely of real life, but by being entirely outside it. We offer ourselves to you unconditionally. (*Beat.*) I don't think you are able to refuse.

The room is silent. Everyone looks at the PRODUCER.

PRODUCER. You really want to play yourself throughout? (*Beat.*) Okay, we'll try it.

ACTRESS. J!

PRODUCER. We'll try it, Fiona, and then we'll see. Can you do it without laughing?

STEPDAUGHTER. Oh, I shan't laugh any more. The nice bit's coming for me now, you'll see.

PRODUCER. Okay, quiet please... and... action. (*To the* FATHER.) So when she said, 'Forget what I said,' you replied, 'I understand, I understand'... something like that?

STEPDAUGHTER (*quietly*). No, he replied, 'Well, then, why don't we just take off your dress?'

Beat.

PRODUCER. Is that really...?

STEPDAUGHTER. It is! You can't trust him. He wants you to piece together a sentimental scene, his little sob story. And to ignore all the reasons why I am what I am. He is to look at me and say, 'Well, let's take off this little dress at once.' And his horrid eyes sparkle. (*Slowly, painfully.*) I think of my father, the only man I have ever known and loved. I think of his cold body in the ground. I try to block out the sound of this creature's heavy breathing. And with my two months' mourning in my heart, and with these fingers tingling with shame... There were others, of course, before this one. But those others mean him for me now. They are all him.

PRODUCER. Can you explain what you mean?

STEPDAUGHTER. The original sin, the most grievous fault, is his. Every crime is now this crime. Because of what he does now, he is responsible for everything else, before and after. Look at him, and see if it isn't true!

The FATHER *is holding his head, sat on the bed amongst the hats. The* MOTHER *begins to moan. The* PRODUCER *gestures to the* CAMERAMAN *to film her. As he does so, from somewhere, a spotlight rises upon her.*

PRODUCER (*to the* MOTHER). You're obviously still haunted by these events of the past?

MOTHER. It is not past. It's happening now, it happens all the time. My torment isn't a pretended one. I live and feel every minute of it. Those two children there – have you heard them speak? They can't talk any more. They cling to me to keep the nightmare actual and vivid. But for themselves, they do not exist, they *aren't*... any more. And she, (*Indicating the* STEPDAUGHTER.) from this moment, will be lost to me. If I now see her here before me, it is only to renew for me the tortures I have suffered for her.

FATHER. The eternal moment! You must catch me, fix me, and hold me for ever in the one fleeting and shameful moment of my life. *Do not spare me.* This is my punishment: the passion in all of us that must culminate in her final cry.

Everyone, by this point, is silent, transfixed. From somewhere music begins to play.

PRODUCER. Stu?

EDITOR (*at the sound-desk, jabbing buttons*). It's not me!

STEPDAUGHTER. I can hear it still in my ears. It's driven me mad, that cry! (*To the* ACTRESS.) You play me any way you like; it doesn't matter. Fully dressed, if you like – provided I have at least one arm bare. One slither of skin for his hand to brush, to clasp...

PRODUCER. What happened next?

The FATHER *moves toward the* STEPDAUGHTER *and grabs her. He kisses her, ripping her dress as he does, and pushes her onto the mattress.*

STEPDAUGHTER. I see a vein pulsing in my arm here; and then, as if that live vein had awakened disgust in me, I close my eyes like this, and let him take me.

The FATHER *and the* STEPDAUGHTER *begin to have sex, as she stares down the camera. This is like a strange, slow dance. The* FATHER *is muttering, chanting in a strange language.*

ACTRESS. J, I think this is... this is awful.

ACTOR. Can we stop now?

The PRODUCER *is transfixed.*

PRODUCER (*to the* MOTHER). And where are you?

MOTHER. On the street outside. I can hear noises...

PRODUCER. And you go in?

MOTHER. And straight upstairs.

PRODUCER. Some part of you suspects what she's doing?

MOTHER. But I couldn't imagine who she's...

The music is building to a crescendo. The FATHER*'s chantings become more and more frenetic and it's impossible to tell if the* STEPDAUGHTER *is writhing in agony or delight.*

PRODUCER. You arrive outside the door!

MOTHER. My heart is racing so fast I think I might faint. I lay a hand on the door.

PRODUCER. Show me!

ACTRESS. J, please stop this!

PRODUCER. Keep filming!

The MOTHER *is behind the door of the set.*

PRODUCER. Go on, go on, what happens next... what happens when you enter?

The MOTHER *enters the room. The* FATHER *and the* STEP-DAUGHTER *turn towards her in surprise. And the music climaxes as horror and recognition spread across the* MOTHER*'s face. A moment of silence. Then she screams. The scream builds until it becomes a high note of pain, which in turn becomes music and she begins to sing; a wailing, operatic lament. She clutches her breast as her aria of grief fills the stunned room. Suddenly the* STEP-DAUGHTER *and the* FATHER *are singing too, loud and fast and getting louder and faster. The music sounds as if an entire orchestra were behind the set. Eventually the music reaches a climax and the three of them freeze.*

PRODUCER. And cut!

Blackout.

End of Act Two.

ACT THREE

On the monitor, the PRODUCER*'s face. She is in the middle of a television interview.*

PRODUCER (*on-screen*). Yes, of course. Of course I've made sacrifices, I'm not ashamed of that. When I began working in television in the early nineties... obviously it was... hard. I've had to fight for every little scrap of success. So, yes, I've made sacrifices, in order to make the work that I think is important. (*Beat.*) I've always believed in the documentary form. In its validity. I believe that good documentaries should be seen as art. I'm an artist and... I'm not ashamed of saying that. I'm an artist and so, for me, the work comes first. I'm not saying that I wouldn't have liked the things that other people – long-term relationships, kids – the things that may be important to other people... but I've consciously chosen something else. (*Pause.*) What happened with my sister... of course it... changed the way I think about lots of things. (*Pause.*) I believe that sometimes there are more important things than thinking about yourself. Documenting other people's lives, telling their stories... well, I've an obligation to my subjects which I take extremely seriously. I choose them, but equally they choose me. So do I think about missing out on those other things? Of course. Do I regret them? (*Pause.*) I've been doing this since I was nineteen and I think I'm addicted to it. I'm a narrative junkie! And like all addicts, I chase my fix, I have to, to follow the story, no matter what the cost to me. The work, (*She gestures at the camera.*) this, it's bigger than me. This isn't my story.

The screen flicks to static and then off. From darkness, howling wind and the MOTHER*'s voice, softly repeating her aria from Act Two.*

FATHER (*in darkness; loudly, to be heard over the wind*).
That's right, over here! Now, if you please, a little light...

*Light and we are outdoors. Or we might be. We are in the
garden of the house we passed in the opening film. To one
side, the edge of a pine forest. Mist and snow swirls violently. The floor is still the floor of the office, but it's dusted
with snow. The fish tank from the first scene is centre stage.
The* CHARACTERS *stand, looking at the* PRODUCER *who
holds a camera.*

PRODUCER. Where are we?

FATHER. The garden. My house. Look, the children recognise
that they're home.

The BOY *and the* GIRL *run from the* MOTHER. *The* GIRL
*goes to the fish tank and looks through it from behind, her
face contorted by the water.*

STEPDAUGHTER. We came back to live here. Do you understand? After that day in the shop, he brought us back. To
make amends, soothe his guilt. Idiotic.

MOTHER. I begged her to forget, (*Gestures to the* FATHER.)
to let him forget. I begged them both to let us become a
family.

STEPDAUGHTER. It's impossible! You old fool. Things like
this don't get forgotten. They fester. The lust doesn't die, it
gets stronger, it feeds on itself. He didn't want me to forget,
he wanted me to remember how it had been. The smell of his
breath on my skin...

FATHER (*desperately*). Please be quiet.

PRODUCER. What do you mean, he wanted you to
remember?

STEPDAUGHTER (*indicating the* SON). And as for him.
Happy families?

SON. Leave me out of this.

STEPDAUGHTER. That's right. Not involved, not implicated. You're such an innocent, aren't you?

PRODUCER. Implicated in what?

STEPDAUGHTER. Things to come.

PRODUCER. What happened after the shop?

FATHER. She told you. Her mother dragged her away from me. I followed them out into the street, begging forgiveness. I could see how they were living, the poverty, so I brought them here with me. (*Pause*.) It could have been better then. Mended. But of course my son resented them being here. Resented what he saw as the invasion of his home.

PRODUCER. How long were they with you?

FATHER. It doesn't matter! You still don't understand? Our story only exists in two moments. Everything else is decoration. One of these moments you've already seen, the moment of my shame. The other, the moment of our tragedy, happens here, in the garden, in the twilight, in the snow. Look.

PRODUCER (*uneasy*). Look at what?

Music. The STEPDAUGHTER *and the* GIRL *are looking into the fishtank, dangling their fingers in the water. The* BOY *stands, letting snow fall between his fingers.*

FATHER. This is the truth. You look at the world through your viewfinder and you see only shadows. Behind you is the fire and the flames flicker. Ignore the shadows, turn around and gaze on the thing itself. Your actors seem to have disappeared. (*Beat*.) Why is there snow here, inside what you still believe to be your production office? Why is there sweat on the back of your neck? Why do you sense something terrible approaching?

PRODUCER. I... I don't understand.

FATHER. It's the simplest thing in the world. Who are you? What are you? What is truth? (*Beat*.) You're frightened.

PRODUCER. A little. Yes.

FATHER. Good. We may be getting somewhere. All the things you believe you can depend on, the tenets by which you live your life, are false. The sooner you admit that we are the purest thing that you have yet encountered, the sooner you will begin to see the truth about yourself.

PRODUCER. What truth? What are you talking about? I thought you said you weren't real?

FATHER. We are more than real. Because we are unchanging, immutable, fixed. Look at us! That fluid realm you call 'reality' has nothing to do with us.

PRODUCER. Look, I just want to know what happens! Why is it so cold in here?

FATHER. Of course. This time of year the weather is terrible. We shouldn't really be outside at this time of day.

PRODUCER. It's the middle of the night! And we're inside.

FATHER. We were, yes. Things are slipping. The rules are changing.

PRODUCER. I just need you to tell me how it ends!

FATHER. Not until you understand. You consider us insane, but we are only what we have been made to be, the creation of another. And no matter how many times our story is told, we are always the same. This mother will always weep, this girl will always laugh, I will remain for ever crucified by guilt. That is what I am.

PRODUCER. So how does that make you real? Or more than real? It makes you imaginary... false!

FATHER. It makes us true! Much more true than the humanity which you celebrate. Think of Oedipus, Emma Bovary... Hamlet! They exist for ever. They're not mere life... they're life plus imagination. As are we. We do not die, we do not age, we do not change. (*Beat.*) Unlike some. But there are other stories being told here. Who are you?

PRODUCER. Me?

FATHER. Yes, who are *you*?

PRODUCER. Well… I'm me.

FATHER. How can you be sure?

PRODUCER. Well… oh, this is ridiculous. I *know* who I am.

FATHER. Really?

PRODUCER. Ask anyone who knows me, ask my friends… ask my crew!

FATHER. They are not here. You're alone. You always have been.

PRODUCER. I've got five hundred names on this phone, ring them!

FATHER. But if I was to call them and they denied all knowledge of you? Would you then cease to exist?

PRODUCER. Of course not… I…

FATHER. Are you defined purely by other people?

PRODUCER. Okay, my passport. I've got it here… (*She searches her pocket.*) Look at the photo…

FATHER. Does the picture resemble you exactly? Exactly as you are now?

PRODUCER. Well, no, it's nearly ten years old. But okay, to see myself, me, I, I just have to look in a mirror and…

FATHER. But what if your appearance changed? (*With a touch of menace.*) What if you were the victim of an accident and were hideously scarred?

PRODUCER. I'd still be me! I'd still have my mind, my memories.

FATHER. Ah, your memories. Look!

On the monitors, home-movie footage of two little girls playing. One has a cardboard box on her head like a helmet. She runs to the camera.

MONITOR (*voice-over*). What do you want to be when you grow up?

PRODUCER (*as a girl, on-screen*). I want to be a spaceman!

PRODUCER. How did you get this?

Now the footage is of a young woman, recognisably the PRODUCER, *ten to fifteen years earlier.*

PRODUCER (*younger, on-screen*). I guess I just think that there are some moral absolutes. And euthanasia is one of them. It's just wrong. We don't get to decide when we die. There are always options and every year medical science provides us with more and more of them. We don't get to decide everything.

FATHER. Why did you change your mind?

PRODUCER (*transfixed by the footage*). I can't remember. (*Beat.*) My sister... got sick. (*Beat.*) She died.

FATHER (*very gently*). You are dying. Every cell of your body. Your skin sloughs off in a million flakes each day, the soft grey tissues of your brain rot and are slowly replaced, the very memories slip away from you like so much water through the sieve of your porous, impermanent skull – and, in a mere seven years, nothing of what you are today will remain.

Pause.

PRODUCER. What's your point?

FATHER. If every word in a book is changed, is it the same book? (*Gestures to the screen.*) That woman, ten years ago, is biologically a completely different creature to the one before me now. There is not a 'you', only a shifting set of vanishing atoms that make up a myriad 'you's. Like your beloved films, you cling to the illusion of a consistent presence – your unchanging truth – but you are no more than twenty-four tiny truths a second – a set of flickering frames in an imitation of life. Yet you deny this fluidity! You cling to

a fixed sense of what is 'real' like a life raft lest you drown.
But you are drowning. You're drowning!

PRODUCER. So what's your...

FATHER. We are what we are for ever, fixed, and this place,
inside or outside, day or night, is the place where our story
exists.

PRODUCER. So what am I doing here?

FATHER. You told the story. You summoned Pace. You recre-
ated the moment between this girl and me. Finish what you
began.

PRODUCER. This is bullshit. I'm leaving.

FATHER. You can't leave. You're involved. This isn't an intellectual exercise. Our existence is now also yours.

The MOTHER *is reaching out to the* SON *and begins to sing
to him. He has his hands over his ears and his eyes closed.
The* FATHER *holds the camera out to the* PRODUCER.

Now we are ready. You want to know how it ends? It's in
your hands.

The PRODUCER *takes the camera, begins to film the*
MOTHER.

PRODUCER. What's she doing?

STEPDAUGHTER. She's imploring him... begging him to
forgive her. Since we moved in, he's shut us out.

SON. *Just be quiet!* This isn't right. This never happened. They
are lying to you!

PRODUCER. What?

SON. She never came to me like this. She never begged.

STEPDAUGHTER. She did! She went to him in the snow, next
to the house, as I sat in the garden, by the pond, with the girl.
(*Gestures to the* BOY.) And him, behind us, always...

watching, plotting. Because he's the sickest of us all, do you understand that?

PRODUCER. The boy?

FATHER. He watches the remains of his infected family consume themselves, with guilt, with sin, and he desperately wants to do something. He wants what we all want. To regain control.

STEPDAUGHTER (*to the* SON). How can you stand there, with your mother imploring you, begging you to forgive her... you heartless bastard, at least look at her!

SON. She never came to me, they're making this up. I was never in the garden... I stayed in my room. No one ever came to me.

FATHER. Lying ingrate! Look at her. Look at us.

The STEPDAUGHTER *crosses to the fishtank and takes the* GIRL*'s hand.*

STEPDAUGHTER. Look, here we are, my darling. Look. My only pleasure is to see her happy and carefree in the garden. So far away from the miserable squalor of the room where we all four slept together.

PRODUCER (*involved*). Before he took you in?

STEPDAUGHTER. At least there's space for us now. A house full of empty rooms, everywhere white. We sleep together now for warmth, do you understand? My contaminated body next to hers, her folding me in her loving little arms.

PRODUCER (*moved*). Of course, your sister loves you.

STEPDAUGHTER. But I still abandon her. I leave her alone time and time again. Alone in the snow.

PRODUCER. Why?

STEPDAUGHTER. For him. Because I want him to want me again. He had me before he knew me, now I want him to have me again, in spite of who I am. In spite of who he is.

PRODUCER. You mean…?

STEPDAUGHTER. He moves us into the house and I become his whore.

FATHER (*in a low whisper*). I try to stop it.

SON. Oh, do you?

FATHER. I promise myself every morning that I'll start afresh. Every time I walk downstairs, it's to embrace my reunited family. And every time my resolve lasts as far as the kitchen door. Look at her. Skin whiter than the snow outside.

Pause.

SON. It gets everywhere.

PRODUCER. What?

SON. The snow. It freezes everything.

PRODUCER. Weren't you at all happy to see your mother?

SON. Happy?

PRODUCER. She'd been away for a long time, now she was back.

SON. She's nothing to me. None of them mean anything to me, but she means least of all. Do you understand that? She's less than nothing.

The MOTHER *howls.*

FATHER. How can you say that?

SON. She abandoned me! They got to live with her… however hard it was, however many of them slept in one room, they got her. I got you.

PRODUCER. But when she comes back, asks you to forgive her…

SON. She never asks! She never apologises. This story you're trying to tell, I don't recognise it! I don't recognise any of this!

PRODUCER. But…

The light slowly begins to change. Sunset.

STEPDAUGHTER. Look! We play by the pond all afternoon. Our mother has left us alone, gone into the house, gone up to his room, begging him to forgive her. The sun begins to set and… I should be watching the children. Instead, I go.

PRODUCER. You go with him?

STEPDAUGHTER. To the forest of pines beyond the lake.

PRODUCER (*quietly*). Is that where you always go?

STEPDAUGHTER. Always.

PRODUCER (*to the* FATHER). The pine forest?

FATHER. What is there to say? I am trapped there for ever. It is too late.

STEPDAUGHTER. Too late for all of us, because of what's about to happen.

FATHER (*calmly*). You can put the camera down now. You'll see there is no longer any need for a barrier between us.

The PRODUCER *lowers the camera.*

STEPDAUGHTER. We're in the pine forest, against a tree. His hands are on me.

FATHER. The mother is with her son, screaming at him to forgive her. He won't even acknowledge her existence.

PRODUCER. Hang on…

SON. This never happened.

STEPDAUGHTER. And no one is by the pond, no one is watching the little ones!

PRODUCER. Wait…

The GIRL *plunges her head into the fish tank.*

PRODUCER. Stop!

STEPDAUGHTER. She falls.

SON. Her mouth gapes.

MOTHER. The water enters her lungs.

FATHER. Her skin begins to turn blue.

SON. I try to escape my mother.

STEPDAUGHTER. He walks out into the snow –

FATHER. – towards the pond –

MOTHER. I'm following him, begging him –

FATHER. – and it's he who sees the girl first –

STEPDAUGHTER. – he stops –

FATHER. – she catches him.

STEPDAUGHTER. And she sees her daughter. She screams and it's her scream – the scream that shook Pace's shop –

FATHER. – the scream in which we are trapped – it's the scream that we hear in the pine forest.

The MOTHER *screams.*

Listen to that!

They come to the fish tank and stop, staring at the GIRL.

PRODUCER. And?! What then? Is she okay? *What then?*

FATHER. This.

They turn slowly to face the BOY, *who steps out of the screen, covered in snow. The* BOY *stares at them, before suddenly producing a large hypodermic syringe from behind his back. In slow motion, he holds it out in front of him, then stabs himself in the heart. He gasps, staggers forward. Blood begins to trickle from his mouth. The needle falls to the floor and the* BOY's *body crumples. The rest of the* CHARACTERS *are still.*

PRODUCER. What's happened?

She walks to the BOY *and reaches down.*

This is real blood, this is real!

FATHER. I repeat the question: what is 'real'? Are you?

PRODUCER. This is real blood! Don't just stand there, do something! *Get some help!* He's dying.

STEPDAUGHTER. What did you think was going to happen? You told the story.

PRODUCER. What? I didn't know that... You begged me to film you!

FATHER. And you have.

The PRODUCER *is trying to make her phone work. She dials. No signal. She tries again. Nothing. She throws the phone away in frustration. She tries to resuscitate the* BOY.

PRODUCER. He's dying.

FATHER. Yes, he is.

STEPDAUGHTER. He always is.

PRODUCER. Then do something!

FATHER. There's nothing more to be done.

The PRODUCER *grabs the camera, but only a snowy static fills the screen. She falls to her knees, and the camera drops. From now on, her physicality is heightened, tragic. After a moment, the* CHARACTERS *walk into the snow and disappear.*

The PRODUCER *crosses to the* BOY *and lifts him, dripping blood. She starts to struggle towards the door. Suddenly the* EDITOR *enters with the* CAMERAMAN *and she falls to her knees.*

PRODUCER. Thank God! Stu! Flor... Help me! Stuart? *Stuart!*

The EDITOR *and the* CAMERAMAN *ignore her completely as they set up the projection screen. The* PRODUCER *tries to grab at them, but they leave.*

Oh fuck… *Stop this!* Please… someone stop this!

She leaves the BOY *on the floor, runs to the door. It is locked. She bang and shouts. Nothing. She returns to the corpse and begins to sob. After a moment or two, with an effort, she falls silent, crawls to the edge of the stage.*

Help me. This is real. I am real… *Please help me!*

Receiving no response, she goes back to the BOY, *lifts him and moves down, off the stage, into the auditorium. She staggers through the theatre, the* BOY *in her arms. Lights dim.*

After a moment the monitors click back on. In a long, single take the camera follows the PRODUCER *through the empty theatre foyer, out into the night. She crosses the car park, struggling with the weight of the* BOY. *She enters and walks through the building opposite. She shouts for help. Eventually she bangs through a door and as it closes behind her we see a sign 'Stage Left. Quiet Please!'*

On stage, a big musical number is being performed, all the cast dancing. The PRODUCER *charges onto stage, carrying the* BOY *in her arms, sobbing and shouting. The cast ignore her, continuing their song. The audience are similarly oblivious. Eventually she runs off the way she came.*

The monitors switch back to static and after several moments the PRODUCER *staggers back onto the stage. She drops the* BOY's *body and turns around. She is confronted by eleven identical copies of herself. She lets out a gasp of fear and turns away. Shaking, she turns back, but the figures have vanished. She flops down next to the* BOY. *After a moment, she picks up the syringe. She shakes her head. Pause. She looks from the* BOY *to the needle. She squirts the syringe and a small jet of liquid fires into the air. Slowly she places the needle against her chest. Breathes deeply. Then she stabs it into her heart. There is a whoosh and she gasps. But she opens her eyes and is alive, the needle sticking out of her chest. In frustration, she begins to stab herself over and over again, each time achieving nothing. She throws the syringe away and, still howling, falls down over the body of the* BOY. *Everything freezes.*

End of Act Three.

ACT FOUR

Everything remains frozen as a large arrow, a cursor, appears. It moves to the top of the screen and illuminates a menu bar. The arrow moves over the word 'MENU' and it flashes.

Blackout. Then, on the screen, slowly fading up and down, still images of moments from the play. Music from earlier. In large letters the words: 'SIX CHARACTERS REMIX: DVD EXTRAS', and a list of options including: 'SUBTITLES', 'LANGUAGE', 'TRAILERS', 'DELETED SCENES' and 'DIRECTOR'S COM-MENTARY'. The arrow moves to the words 'DIRECTOR'S COMMENTARY: ON?' and again it flashes. It moves to the words 'PLAY FROM START', flashes. Blackout.

The stage has been reset. We now see again the action of Act One from the beginning, every move replicated. Clearly audible to the audience over the top of the stage dialogue are two new voices (in the right-hand column).

A large projection screen. On it, a film of a bleak Danish land-scape, which gradually becomes a suburban town. We pass a large, nondescript house, to one side a clutch of pine trees.

PRODUCER (*voice-over, mid-sentence with film*).
…the drive from Copen-hagen airport takes over three hours, but the waiting is at long last over and Andrew arrives at the clinic.

Cut to a middle-aged woman with a Danish accent talking to camera.

LULLY. The final session is always an intense moment

for both the patient and all our team at Dignitas.

We see the family move through a waiting room. In the background we see another family, dressed in black, also waiting. The hospital is very clean – pine and pot plants. Occasionally we see outside through huge glass windows.

(*Voice-over.*) I wake on these days with a, how d'you say, a... *felag...*

PRODUCER (*voice-over*). Sharper?

LULLY (*voice-over*). Yes. Exactly, a sharper sense of life itself, no? Those days when we are all more in focus – the vividness of the colours in the sky here, the crisp bite of the air.

We see ANDREW *sitting at the end of a corridor with his* MOTHER, *but at a distance and in shadow.*

It is a special moment every time. We prepare the room, the bed linen, the lighting, yes, even the injection itself with great consideration and – tenderness, you understand?

DIRECTOR (*voice-over*). Hello.

WRITER (*voice-over*). Hello.

DIRECTOR (*voice-over*). And welcome to the *Six Characters Remix Director's Commentary*. This is an attempt from me, the director...

WRITER (*voice-over*)....and me, the writer and editor, to describe the aims of the film and some of the techniques we've tried to use in making it.

Even more so for a child,
of course.

We see a NURSE *place a
needle on a bedside table.*
ANDREW*'s schoolbag
next to the bed. Another
shot of* ANDREW'S
FATHER *looking at a
graveyard. Cut to*
ANDREW*'s empty
bedroom in Macclesfield,
his toys on the floor. Cut
back to Denmark and a
sudden flock of birds on the
horizon. Cut back to*
LULLY, *dabbing at her
eye. Tears.*

I'm sorry. (*Looking away.*)
I'm so sorry…

*Image freezes. Lights up as
at the start of Act One. The
voices of the* PRODUCER
*and her film-crew are
quieter than before.*

PRODUCER. So…

EXEC. Okay… I wonder if…

PRODUCER. Actually, wait.
Stu, just lay the track on so
Bob can get a better sense
of…

EDITOR. Sure. Any bit in
partic…?

PRODUCER. No, just the
theme.

DIRECTOR (*voice-over*).
Right from the top, we put
a lot of time and resources
into making the Dignitas
film feel authentic.

WRITER (*voice-over*). We
needed the world of Joanna
and her crew to feel as
realistic as possible.

DIRECTOR (*voice-over*).
That's why getting an
actress as good as Anna-
Maria felt really vital to
pulling it off. I think she's
brilliant here… even
though everything she does
is totally naturalistic,
you're always aware that
she's acting and… there's a
kind of pleasure in that.

DIRECTOR (*voice-over*). So
now we're into the live
scene and the abandoned
office the film-makers are
working in.

The whole film plays again, this time softly scored with a spare, plaintive piece of music.

PRODUCER (*voice-over, mid sentence with film*). …the drive from Copenhagen airport takes over three hours, but the waiting is at long last over and Andrew arrives at the clinic.

Cut to a middle-aged woman with a Danish accent talking to camera.

LULLY. The final session is always an intense moment for both the patient and all our team at Dignitas.

We see the family move through a waiting room. The hospital is very clean – pine and pot plants. Occasionally we see outside through huge glass windows. The second family in black are absent from the film this time.

(*Voice-over.*) I wake on these days with a, how d'you say, a… *felag*…

PRODUCER (*voice-over*). Sharper?

LULLY (*voice-over*). Yes. Exactly, a sharper sense of life itself, no? Those days

WRITER (*voice-over*). We were going to make it clearer that the film crew were on location in Denmark in our final cut…

DIRECTOR (*voice-over*). …i.e. they're not in some swish Soho edit suite like the one we're in now.

WRITER (*voice-over*). But we had to cut all that stuff out because there just wasn't room for everything…

DIRECTOR (*voice-over*). …right. And also, although every character is important to us, the whole edit backstory is of course only a red herring, a set-up for the introduction of the characters that comes later.

when we are all more in focus – the vividness of the colours in the sky here, the crisp bite of the air.

We see ANDREW *sitting at the end of a corridor with his* MOTHER, *but at a distance and in shadow.*

It is a special moment every time. We prepare the room, the bed linen, the lighting, yes, even the injection itself with great consideration and – tenderness, you understand? Even more so for a child, of course. We dream of our perfect wedding, so also we plan our perfect end. This is what we offer, even in cases as tragic as this.

The same sequence of images.

I'm sorry. (*Looking away.*) I'm so sorry.

On the screen a symbol 'x 16' is seen. Everyone on stage moves through twenty seconds of fast-forward. Film whizzes by on the monitors.

Normal speed resumes.

EXEC. ...And the whole story, the entire thing, hinged on that one

DIRECTOR (*voice-over*). This musical theme, which Adam had from the very start, was crucial in guiding us towards the whole aural landscape of the piece...

WRITER (*voice-over*). Can we skip forward a moment?

– I just want to look at the Exec's exit.

moment, just suddenly from nowhere, it was extraordinary…

PRODUCER. It was. I know.

EXEC. And there in one moment we had the whole story and, not only that, we had an ending – a fucking gold-plated, BAFTA-munching, fuck-you-too-Yentob ending!

PRODUCER. I know.

EXEC. Here we have a great ending, I mean, the kid is dead! I know, forgive me… But where's the coverage?

PRODUCER. I know.

EXEC. Look, J. J. I know you. I know you're not like the others.

PRODUCER. Thanks. I mean, which others?

EXEC. Greengrass. Loach. All those arseholes… Fucking off to drama as soon as they could. 'Auteurs.'

ACTRESS. I love Loach.

EXEC. Of course you do. You're an actor. But this is Factual and we do it a bit differently here, keep it

WRITER (*voice-over*). There's no doubt that the Jonze/Kaufman films were in our heads whilst we were writing the movie –

– but there were a lot of influences, and some of them might be slightly harder to spot.

DIRECTOR (*voice-over*). Well, Lars von Trier –

WRITER (*voice-over*). – Yes…

DIRECTOR (*voice-over*). – particularly *Dogville*, I suppose, and *Kingdom*,

real. The mirror up to nature, yes?

ACTRESS. I'm just saying that...

EXEC. Look J, J, just keep, keep digging! I mean, just follow your hunch, your nose. We can't afford for this to be sterile... dull, to be frank. We've already spent a lot – a lot! – of money out here. Just remember, it's a series of personal films; secret histories, things you'd never find on your normal 'Sex and the Third Reich' channels – the cutting edge, yes?

PRODUCER. Sure.

EXEC (*quietly*). Look, I know you've got a lot invested in this, J – personally, I mean. It was your sister, wasn't it, who was ill for a long time?

PRODUCER. Yes.

EXEC. Yes. Well... I know it will come together if you just free it up a bit – make it matter more. It's all about access, remember.

PRODUCER. Of course.

EXEC. Anyway, I've got to be on a plane in a couple of

the horror-hospital TV series...

WRITER (*voice-over*). Yes.

DIRECTOR (*voice-over*). The whole Danish setting, really, was inspired by the aesthetic of several European film-makers... but particularly von Trier, Haneke...

WRITER. So here's the emergence of the 'sister' subplot...

hours, but I'll call when I'm back in the office and we can talk more. Okay?

PRODUCER. Sure.

EXEC. See where we're at, eh? Okay. Catch you guys later. It's great work.

He breezes out. Beat.

ACTOR. Access?

EDITOR. He's right. If we don't get more personal testimony we're fucked. We might as well have made a bloody docu-drama.

ACTRESS. I thought this was a docu-drama?

EDITOR. No, no, no, no. This is a drama-documentary.

Beat.

ACTOR. Sorry, what is the difference between a docu-drama and a drama-docu-mentary?

EDITOR. A drama-doc is what we're doing – a docu-mentary with some dra-matic reconstructions, whereas a docu-drama is a scripted film of real-life events.

ACTRESS. Like *Bloody Sunday*.

DIRECTOR (*voice-over*). The suggestion is that already Joanna has an emotional relationship to the euthanasia storyline...

DIRECTOR (*voice-over*). It was crucial to me that the film-makers – Joanna, the producer, and her actors – were vividly real.

WRITER (*voice-over*). Again, the Dogme school was a kind of model for the idea of a film-making collec-tive, what Joanna describes as a 'democracy'.

PRODUCER. Exactly.

ACTOR. So why aren't we just making this as a docu-drama? Lose the real-life stuff and just use recon-struction?

PRODUCER. Because we don't have the budget and because I still believe that real people have something, a texture, an authenticity...

Everything freezes and the pause sign appears.

A loud knock.

DIRECTOR (*voice-over*). Oh bollocks. Press pause.

WRITER (*voice-over*). Who the hell is that?

Knocking.

DIRECTOR (*voice-over*). Hang on.

WRITER (*voice-over*). I think we're locked in.

DIRECTOR (*voice-over*). Here, I've got a keycard thing.

Knocking.

WRITER (*voice-over*). Hang on, I'm coming!

The sound of a door opening.

FATHER (*voice-over*). Excuse me...

Lights rise on an office upstage, the PRODUCER *back in
her position from the end of Act Three, cradling the* BOY.
The EDITOR *and the* ACTORS *have left. In the rear office
we see the* EXEC, *who has suddenly lost his odd goatee
beard. With him are two* THEATRE-MAKERS, A *and* B.
They are in mid-flow…

THEATRE-MAKER A. …and so it cuts away from the whole
Director's Commentary idea just as we realise who it is at
the door.

EXEC. The father's voice?

THEATRE-MAKER B. Exactly, just a word or two. Just
enough to identify him. So the whole thing's been hijacked
and, again, we're on a different level of reality.

THEATRE-MAKER A. We thought the DVD commentary was
the bottom line, the truth, but no! The characters are too
powerful, they're in there too! Like a virus, they're
spreading now they've been released!

EXEC. Nice. Bit of a gimmick, of course, but a nice one.

THEATRE-MAKER A. In the spirit of the Pirandello, though –
we think.

THE EXEC (*chuckling*). Director's Commentary. Okay. (*Beat.*)
Well, I think it's ambitious.

THEATRE-MAKER B. Too much?

EXEC. I don't think so. I'm sick of these slavish, academic
translations. We got rid of them in film and telly years ago.
It's not like the original isn't there to be faithfully performed
afterwards. No, I like it. Clever. So is it a big budget, do you
think? Big set?

THEATRE-MAKER B. Not at all. It's a really lo-fi world. A
kind of postmodern neutral space. We actually really like
your office.

EXEC. What. This one?

THEATRE-MAKER A. No, the one across the hall.

They move into the main stage area.

EXEC. This one? But there's nothing here – it's waiting for a refurb.

THEATRE-MAKER B. Yeah, we love it. The leftover furniture, the crap all over the floor. We even thought we might keep the fish tank. It's kind of creepy.

THEATRE-MAKER A. Yeah, it's exactly the kind of banal environment that's a shorthand in contemporary European theatre for postmodern alienation. Very cool, you know?

EXEC. But it's just an empty office.

THEATRE-MAKER A. But people will read it as much more than that in a theatre. It's a metaphor.

EXEC. Okay, whatever you guys think. Sounds a bit grim to me, but if you say that's 'in' now, then... and I guess it'll be cheap. Whatever you say.

THEATRE-MAKER B. So obviously, we were hoping to get it on this year –

THEATRE-MAKER A. – because we know the National are planning one and if they do it, that'll blow us out of the water.

EXEC. Hmm. Well, the money is there, though as you know we haven't invested in a show before.

THEATRE-MAKER B. But we thought, with your links to the Pirandello estate –

THEATRE-MAKER A. – and the overlap of subject matter... you know, TV-makers...

THEATRE-MAKER B. You felt like the right guy.

EXEC. Well, when you first mentioned it to me, I thought it sounded absolutely right for us... and I certainly like the sound of this arsehole Exec Producer in the first scene.

(*Chuckles.*) I guess the biggest question will inevitably be casting. I was talking about it to Julia and she asked if you guys had anyone in mind yet?

THEATRE-MAKER B. To be honest, I'm not sure. It feels a little early for that, but, I mean, if your involvement is dependent on getting a name, then there are some people…

EXEC. No, no, don't worry about casting. I'll leave that to the pros. Consider us in. Just make sure you get someone bloody dashing to play the Executive Producer!

THEATRE-MAKER A. Brilliant.

THEATRE-MAKER B. We'll do our best.

EXEC. Shall I call Rome right now? Get things moving in terms of copyright?

THEATRE-MAKER B. That'd be great.

EXEC. You know, Pirandello did about six different versions, I mean, he never left the thing alone, so we need to be clear which one we're getting authorisation for.

THEATRE-MAKER A. In a way it doesn't matter. I mean, our translation is so free…

EXEC. Sure, but the estate can be fussy. (*Into a mobile.*) Jenni, could you get me Signor Dellafiore, please? (*Back to the others.*) I think it's going to be great, you know. What about a West End transfer?

THEATRE-MAKER B. Well, we'd obviously love to…

EXEC. Ah, sorry. (*Into phone.*) Giacomo? Bob Gibson… (*Louder.*) Bob Gibson! (*Louder.*) *Si*, Bob!… *Come sta?… Molto bene, molto bene… bellissima…* Giacomo, I have a question for you about the Pirandello foreign-performance rights?… Uh-huh… Yeah, because a couple of friends of mine want to do a new version of *Sei Personaggi*… Er, Chichester… On the south coast… Well, they'd like to get in before the National… Ha!… Thing is, they want to do a bit of a number on it. Let me sketch it out. Instead of being

about a theatre rehearsal, it's about this female film-maker...
I know... She's in Denmark...

As the EXEC *is speaking, the* FATHER *and the*
STEPDAUGHTER *close the blinds on the room and then
enter like Bonnie and Clyde. She stands to one side as he
reveals an enormous meat cleaver. As the* EXEC *continues
to describe the show down the telephone, the* FATHER
steps behind the two THEATRE-MAKERS *and begins to
butcher them both. His movements are enormous, ritualistic
– the moment feels sacrificial. Blood spurts everywhere,
including all over the oblivious* EXEC, *who blithely continues describing the concept of the show. As the* FATHER
hacks them to pieces, the MOTHER, *the* SON *and the*
GIRL *enter. There is a knock at the door. The* EXEC *goes
to open it but there is no one there. He walks down the hall
and off. From another door enters* LUIGI PIRANDELLO.
*He carries a large exercise book and a pen. He is dressed
in 1925 clothes. He sits at a table and starts to write –
though this is clearly a struggle. The lights soften and we
hear sounds of a late-evening garden outside, perhaps the
strains of an old Puccini gramophone record. His*
HOUSEKEEPER *enters carrying an oil-lamp. Momentarily
they are still like a Vermeer painting. The* PRODUCER
numbly watches, still with the BOY. *The* HOUSEKEEPER
and PIRANDELLO *start to talk in Italian, but subtitles are
provided on the screens.*

HOUSEKEEPER. The pasta is on the table, sir. We will eat
now.

PIRANDELLO. Nothing for me, thank you, Amalia.

HOUSEKEEPER. Mr Pirandello, you must eat something.
You've been writing for hours.

PIRANDELLO. But getting nowhere, I'm afraid. (*Sighs.*) Hon-
estly, I despair of this play, I despair!

HOUSEKEEPER. But why?

PIRANDELLO. It's just... impossible.

HOUSEKEEPER. But the first act is so funny, so original. The characters bursting in like that. The mother in mourning! It's hilarious.

PIRANDELLO. But I can't seem to find an ending. Days now, staring at the page. I think I must give up and return to novels.

HOUSEKEEPER. Nonsense. I won't hear of it.

PIRANDELLO. I look at these words and they seem dead, lifeless to me. They're like etchings on a gravestone – attempts to describe life, but stillborn.

HOUSEKEEPER. I won't hear it. This is your masterpiece. Your symphony.

PIRANDELLO. An unfinished symphony. The characters – I woke one morning to find them fully formed next to me, demanding my attention. The girl in particular, screeching her head off. Insisting on my efforts, but now I can't put them to bed. They just don't seem to want to lie down and behave.

PIRANDELLO *laughs bitterly.*

HOUSKEEPER (*touching him, gently*). Come and eat with us. Something will come up. I know you, sir. A leaf falls and – voilà, inspiration! Come to dinner. Little Giacomo is visiting and I know how you enjoy his company. Come to dinner, sir. I'm serving venison...

PIRANDELLO. Very well, dear Amalia. My characters can wait. How can I resist your venison?

They exit together. As they leave, the FATHER *and the* STEPDAUGHTER *enter. They take positions to replicate the Vermeer composition of the* HOUSEKEEPER *and* PIRANDELLO. *The* FATHER *writes quickly and certainly in the book and then folds it shut. He looks at the still-prone* PRODUCER *who has watched all this in silence. The* FATHER *looks at the* STEPDAUGHTER *as* HAMLET *appears.*

HAMLET. O, what a rogue and peasant slave am I!
    Is it not monstrous that this player here,
    But in a fiction, in a dream of passion,
    Could force his soul so to his own conceit
    That from her working all his visage wann'd,
    Tears in his eyes, distraction in's aspect,
    A broken voice, and his whole function suiting
    With forms to his conceit? And all for nothing!

HAMLET fades to darkness and the PRODUCER *takes over the speech.*

PRODUCER. What would he do,
    Had he the motive and the cue for passion
    That I have? He would drown the stage with tears
    And cleave the general ear with horrid speech,
    Make mad the guilty and appal the free,
    Confound the ignorant, and amaze indeed
    The very faculties of eyes and ears. Yet I,
    A dull and muddy-mettled rascal, peak,
    Like John-a-dreams, unpregnant of my cause,
    And can say nothing.

Upstage in the rear office the lights fade up. It is now an exact replica of the Dignitas clinic. The FATHER *and the* STEPDAUGHTER *assemble in white coats. The* STEPDAUGHTER *takes up the syringe from the bedside table. The* PRODUCER *puts down the* BOY, *walks into the rear office and slips into the bed. The* FATHER *hands her the syringe and the* CHARACTERS *gather around the bed. The* PRODUCER *injects herself and falls asleep.*

An End.